Botswana:
A Short Political History

STUDIES IN AFRICAN HISTORY
General Editor: A. H. M. Kirk-Greene
St Antony's College
Oxford

ANTHONY SILLERY

BOTSWANA
A Short Political History

METHUEN & CO LTD
11 New Fetter Lane · London EC4

First published 1974 by Methuen & Co Ltd
© *1974 Anthony Sillery*
Printed in Great Britain by
Richard Clay (The Chaucer Press), Ltd,
Bungay, Suffolk

ISBN 0 416 75480 5   hardback
ISBN 0 416 75650 6   paperback

Distributed in the USA
by HARPER & ROW PUBLISHERS, INC.
BARNES & NOBLE IMPORT DIVISION

Contents

Acknowledgements

To those in Britain and Africa who patiently answered my questions, gave me advice and supplied me with information on aspects of the subject with which I was insufficiently familiar, I offer heartfelt thanks.

My wife and I are particularly grateful to our friends in Botswana whose kindness and hospitality during our return visit to Gaborone in Autumn 1972 made this one of our happiest memories.

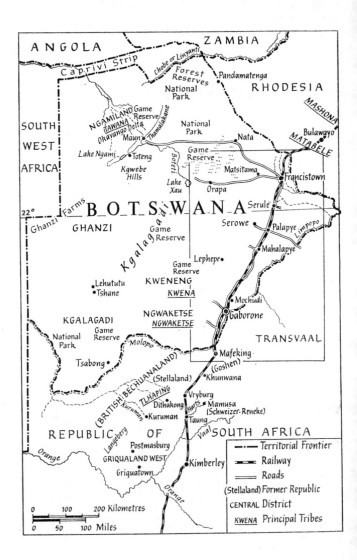

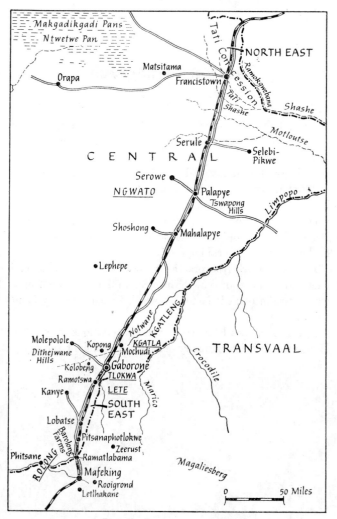

Detail of map on p. viii.

Note on Orthography

African names are spelt in the modern way: Setshele not Sechele, Sekgoma not Sekhoma. The exception is Khama, which in deference to the style adopted by that family I spell in the old way.

As is usual nowadays I drop the Bantu prefix: Tswana not Batswana, Kwena not Bakwena, Ngwato not Bamangwato. The form Matabele or Matebele is so common that any other would seem strange and I therefore preserve it. I also keep Basuto for the people of Basutoland (Lesotho) because Suto or Sotho has a wider meaning (p. 7).

It was formerly the practice to give the value of a semi-consonant to certain vowels in combination: ea = ya, oa = wa. A case in point is Montsioa, which I spell correctly Mont-shiwa.

For place names I follow the recommendations of the Place Names Commission (Ministry of Local Government and Lands, 1970).

A. S.

I · Country and People

'Being now informed by the guides that the distance to the residence of their Chief was only a short day's journey, it was considered expedient to halt the waggons, while the two commissioners should proceed on horseback. Accordingly having selected a present for the Chief, which they carried in knapsacks and their pistol holsters, they set out with an interpreter; and about the middle of the day, after passing through open fields that for a very considerable extent were under a rude sort of cultivation, they entered a large town. . . . The sight of so great an assemblage of human habitations, after so long and dreary a journey, was equally as unexpected as it was agreeable.'[1]

The year was 1801 and the commissioners were Pieter Jan Trüter and Dr William Somerville, who had been sent to the interior by the Government of the Cape Colony to procure draught oxen to replace local stocks depleted by drought. The town which made such an agreeable impression on the visitors was Dithakong, some forty miles north-east of the Kuruman (properly Kudumane) river and roughly a hundred miles south of the present southern boundary of Botswana. It was the capital of the Tlhaping, the southernmost member of the Tswana group of tribes, and in 1801 it was a town of ten to fifteen thousand inhabitants.* The chief, whose name was Molehabangwe, received the visitors 'without the least embarrassment, and in the most friendly manner', while his people seemed

---

* Dithakong, written even by missionaries who knew the language as Lattakoo, Litako, and in other inaccurate ways, means 'place of stone walls'. The name is derived from the ancient stone cattle kraals which are a feature of the district (P.-L. Breutz, *The Tribes of Vryburg District*).

delighted to see the strangers: 'Many of them were extremely curious, but without being troublesome, and all of them perfectly good humoured.'[2] The report of the commissioners is the earliest firsthand account that we have of the Tswana,[3] and it is made all the more valuable by the illustrations of local life by the artist Samuel Daniell, who accompanied the expedition. (The commissioners' report, originally written in Dutch by Trüter, is somewhat incongruously, but for good reason, included as a 'supplementary article' in John Barrow's *Voyage to Cochin-China*.)

The commissioners found an orderly community living in some comfort and elegance with a mixed economy in which cattle predominated. 'The *Booshuanas*', says their report, 'are arrived at that stage of civilization which is not satisfied with the mere necessaries of life supplied to them abundantly from the three sources of agriculture, grazing, and hunting; they are by no means insensible of its conveniencies and its luxuries.'[4] The 'regularity and decorum' with which these peaceable and happy people conducted themselves on all occasions was noted by the commissioners, who drew from their observations a 'complete refutation' of the opinion 'that has industriously been inculcated' that the unalterable lot of Africans was to be slaves.

Trüter and Somerville were followed by other travellers, who met the same friendly hospitality as their predecessors. 'As I passed along among the numerous inhabitants of this populous town,' wrote Henry Lichtenstein of his visit in 1805, 'and met frequently a face that I knew, my heart felt a secret delight that fate had appointed me, in preference to so many others, to visit a nation so well worthy of attention'.[5]

The naturalist W. J. Burchell, seven years later, was less ecstatic but like the commissioners of 1801 he pays a generous tribute to the social discipline of his hosts. 'These people', he says, 'are, in common society, exceedingly well ordered, and conduct themselves with a remarkably careful attention to decorum in several respects.'[6] He does however condemn a general vice of begging, especially for tobacco and snuff, from which even the notables were not exempt.

From these accounts of travellers we gain the impression of a lively and well-ordered society, hospitable to strangers though aware of the advantages to be won from visitors, with skills in a number of crafts and with a special gift for domestic architecture.

It was indeed the houses of the Tlhaping that particularly struck the European visitors. Lichtenstein comments on their 'commodiousness and durability'.[7] 'There is one quality', says Burchell,

> for which the Bachapins, and probably the other tribes of Bichuanas, are greatly to be admired, and in which they excel all the more southern inhabitants of this part of Africa; the neatness, good order and cleanness of their dwellings. Nothing can exceed their *neatness*; and by *cleanness* I mean to say, the great carefulness which they show to remove all rubbish and every thing unsightly: not a twig, nor a loose pebble, nor dust, nor even a straw, is to be seen on the floor within the fence; nothing lies out of its place, and it is evident that in the better houses they are continually attending to these circumstances. The houses of the poorer people are not so remarkable for this care; but still they exhibit much neatness.[8]

Their method of storing corn and beans was equally remarkable, showing 'a degree of ingenuity equal to that which is displayed in the construction of their houses, and is to be admired for its simplicity and perfect adequateness to the purpose'.[9]

The personal appearance of the people was seemly and elegant. Dress was dignified and simple. The men's principal garment was the *kobo*, a cloak made from leather or from fur. Poor people wore antelope skins, but the rich wore cloaks made from the finer skins of jackals, wild cats and other animals. The women wore several aprons, one over the other. 'The inner one has a number of strips of leather sewed to the bottom, forming a sort of fringe, which moving about as they walk, keeps the flies from their legs.'[10]

The Tlhaping were much given to self-adornment with ivory, brass, and copper ornaments and rings, and they smeared the body with an ointment compounded of grease and a shiny metallic powder called *sibilo* which, says Burchell, 'is quite as becoming as our own hair-powder, and is a practice not more unreasonable than ours'.[11]

These picturesque and comfortable fashions later fell under the ban of the missionaries and gave way to the more godly shirt and trousers and Mother Hubbard.

It would perhaps be wrong to read too much into the accounts of travellers, however percipient, to whom the discovery of a friendly people living in seclusion and untouched by the outside world was itself an enchantment. But it certainly seems that at that time the Tlhaping, apart from tiffs with their neighbours the Rolong, were indeed enjoying a period of peace and of such prosperity as their environment allowed. It was not, as we shall see, a state of affairs that was destined to last for long.

The region with which we shall be mainly concerned is roughly that which extends northwards from the Orange river to the Zambezi. The eastern boundary is formed by the Limpopo (Crocodile) river in the north and by the Vaal and Harts rivers in the south. The western boundary has no significance in the early stages of the narrative, but it can be taken to lie along longitude 21° as far south as latitude 22°, and from there southwards along longitude 20°.

Politically the scene is divided into two parts. Southern Bechuanaland, once the colony of British Bechuanaland, has long been part of the Cape Province of the Republic of South Africa. The territory lying north of the Molopo is the Republic of Botswana, formerly the Bechuanaland Protectorate. At the extreme eastern end, where the road and the railway cross from the Republic of South Africa, the boundary is the Ramatlabama stream, a tributary of the Molopo. The total area of the region is 274,000 square miles, of which Botswana accounts for 223,000.

This region is for the most part rolling tableland with an average altitude of 3300 ft above sea level. The eastern side is broken by rocky hills and river valleys, and in southern Bechuanaland there is hilly country south of Kuruman. West of Postmasburg the Langeberg mountains run down towards the Orange river. The western side of the region is the Kgalagadi desert, an expanse of undulating sandbelts and limestone out-crops, with a cover of grass and thorn scrub. In some areas where water is nearer to the surface the Kgalagadi resembles parkland, but typical desert conditions prevail in the south-west, where there is little vegetation and sand dunes occur.

The region suffers over most of its area from a lack of per-manent surface water. In the remote north-west the Okavango river enters Botswana from Angola and forms a great inland delta, a fascinating landscape of luxuriant vegetation with broad expanses of water studded with wooded islands. Much of the Okavango flow is trapped in the swamps and evaporates, but at flood time it overspills into Lake Ngami and into the Makgadikgadi salt lake, where in due course it also disappears. Apart from the peripheral Limpopo, Chobe and Zambezi, the Okavango is the only important source of permanent water in Botswana, though large standing pools remain in other rivers for some time after the rains. To supplement the lack of surface water the people have recourse to dams, boreholes and pits in sand rivers.

Apart from one natural phenomenon, the Kuruman river within a few miles of its source, which will be described later (p. 16), the picture in southern Bechuanaland is much the same. In general permanent water for man and beast is only obtained by human labour, by damming, boring and digging.

True forest does not occur, but there is a reasonable imitation in a stretch of savannah woodland near the Chobe river which

is commonly described as forest. This furnishes a number of
exploitable timber trees such as *mokusi* (*Baikiaea Plurijuga*),
mokwa (*Pterocarpus Angolensis*), and *mwande* (*Afzelia Cuan-
zensis*). Outside the forest zone in the north and north-west there
are great tracts of *mopane* (*Colophospermum mopane*), a tree of
little or no economic value, but with a pretty leaf that resembles a butterfly when it falls. The *mogonono* (*terminalia sericea*)
and *mosetlha*, a kind of acacia, are widespread. In some tribes
it was forbidden to cut these while the crops were growing, as
it was commonly held that this would cause destructive hail
storms. So in a small way superstition comes to the help of the
conservationist!

The climate is generally sub-tropical, but varies according to
the locality. During the winter, which lasts from May until
August, the days are warm and the nights cold, with occasional
storms. August is a windy month, when sand-storms sweep
across the country from the Kgalagadi. The rains begin, or
should begin, in October and last till April, and this period is
usually hot, but not oppressively so. Rainfall is highest on the
eastern side, where it reaches 27″ annually. In this better-
watered area the soil is more productive and there are wide
stretches of good grazing. It is therefore here that the greater
part of the population lives. In the central and western areas
the rains are scanty, dwindling to 8″ and sometimes considerably less. These areas are inhabited by people who congregate
round the larger water holes and supplement their insecure
pastoral economy by collecting and hunting. Over the whole
region rain is highly unreliable, and droughts are frequent even
on the eastern side, making agriculture a discouraging occupation. It is not for nothing that the ceremonial Tswana greeting
is *Pula*, rain.

The Tswana, of whom the Tlhaping are part, are one of the
three divisions of the Sotho group of the Bantu family. The
other two divisions are the Southern Sotho, more commonly

called Basuto, of Lesotho, and the Northern Sotho, tribes like the Pedi, who live in the northern Transvaal. The Tswana are sometimes called Western Sotho. The name Tswana has appeared in a number of forms, for instance Booshuana, as in the Trüter–Somerville report, and also Bootchuana, Bichuana, Beetjuans, but it became standardized as Bechuana, whence Bechuanaland, of which Botswana is an exact translation.

Tswana is the most widely dispersed Bantu language in southern Africa, being spoken by the predominant tribes in Botswana, southern Bechuanaland, the western Transvaal, and in parts of the Orange Free State. Over so vast an area there are naturally dialectal variations, but in general the language is surprisingly uniform throughout the Tswana field. In addition to those to whom Tswana is the mother tongue, there are thousands of people in Botswana who use Tswana as a second language.[12]

The origins of the Sotho, like those of most African tribes, are shrouded in legend. The accepted theory is that they came from the north at the time of the Bantu migrations into southern Africa, the first to arrive being the Kgalagadi, who settled in the eastern part of modern Botswana, mingling with the aboriginal Bushmen. The next were the people now represented by the Rolong and their offshoots, whose first home was along the upper reaches of the Molopo river, from where they spread south and west. Finally, with the last and greatest wave of migration, came the ancestors of all the other Sotho tribes. These settled at first in the south-west Transvaal, then in the course of centuries spread in a broad belt across the middle of southern Africa from Lesotho to Botswana. On the western fringe the Kgalagadi gave way before the later migrations and retreated to the desert that bears their name.

According to tradition the Tswana forming part of this last wave were originally a united people, but they soon broke up into different tribes. Fragmentation has been a recurring feature of Tswana history, each section as it hived off moving to

another locality where it would set up under a new chief. Thus
the Kgatla and the Kwena are early offshoots of the Hurutshe,
said to have been the leaders of the final migration. Then the
Kgatla and the Kwena themselves divided into other tribes as
time went on. Of the earlier wave the Tlhaping are a secessionist
offshoot of the Rolong, as are the Maidi and the Kaa;* and the
Rolong, who were once united under one chief, are now four
separate tribes.

From our point of view the most important of these tribal
divisions took place about 1720, when a group of Kwena under
a leader named Kgabo separated from the parent stem in the
western Transvaal and came to live in the Dithejwane hills near
the present town of Molepolole. The Ngwato and the Ngwaketse
were still at that time part of Kgabo's Kwena but they soon
hived off in turn to form independent tribes. There was another
secession about 1795 when Tawana, son of the reigning chief of
the Ngwato, broke away with a band of followers and went first
to the Boteti river then to the Kgwebe hills in Ngamiland, there
to found a tribe named Tawana after him.

There are now eight principal tribes in Botswana, of whom
four, the Kwena, Ngwato, Ngwaketse and Tawana, are descendants of Kgabo's migration. Of these the Kwena are tradition-
ally regarded as the senior, with the Ngwato and the Ngwaketse
following in that order. Other tribes were added during the nineteenth century: the Kgatla, who came in 1871; the Tlokwa, a
small section of a much larger group of that name in other parts
of South Africa; and the Lete, not Tswana but Transvaal
Ndebele who have completely assimilated Tswana culture. The
eighth is the Rolong, who claim an ancestry more remote than
any, and who live partly in Botswana and partly in the Cape
Province, on either side of the Molopo river.

The eight principal tribes do not by any means constitute the
whole African population of Botswana. To these nuclear com-

---

* The Kaa live in Botswana. The other Rolong offshoots are in the Cape
Province of South Africa.

munities are affiliated other tribes, who for one reason or another have accepted the rule of the chief of the principal tribe and have become his subjects. Some of these affiliated tribes, such as the Kaa, are of Tswana origin. Others, like the Tswapong, are Northern Sotho. The Kgalagadi, as we have seen, are descended from the earliest Sotho migration. Others, for instance the Yei or Koba and Mbukush of Ngamiland and the

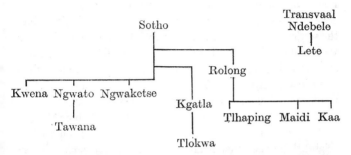

Talaote who live in Ngwato country are not Sotho at all, but of quite different origin. In the southern part of Botswana the affiliated tribes form a comparatively small part of the population, but among the Ngwato and the Tawana in the north and north-west they far outnumber the principal tribe of the area. Nor are these dependent communities each necessarily resident wholly under one chief. Several are scattered about among different tribes according to the vagaries of their history.

The oldest race in Botswana is that of the Bushmen, regarded as the aboriginal inhabitants of most of southern Africa, but now virtually confined to Botswana, South-West Africa and Angola. They are small, yellow or yellowish-brown in colour, with narrow eyes, prominent cheekbones and very flat noses. One of their more notable characteristics is the tendency to accumulate masses of fat on the buttocks.

In Botswana the home of the Bushmen is the Kgalagadi, where they live in small groups as hunters and gatherers, neither practising agriculture nor keeping cattle. In spite of this precarious way of life they are a merry people, much given to dancing and singing. Above all they have produced a remarkable form of art, the rock-paintings, scenes of people and animals and everyday activities painted in vivid colours on the rock walls of caves. The art has now quite died out, and many of the paintings that we see today must be very old.

Silberbauer calculated that the number of Bushmen in Bechuanaland in 1964 was 24,652, with a 20 per cent margin of error. Of these, three-quarters were more or less assimilated into the settled communities, European and African, while about six thousand continued to live the old nomadic life, hunting game and gathering edible plants and roots.[13] The 1971 census gives an estimated figure of 10,550 for 'nomads not enumerated'. The word 'nomad' here means Bushmen and Kgalagadi.

The total population of Botswana is 630,000 of whom 98·1 per cent are Tswana (the word here denotes nationality, not tribal origin).[14] On the other hand there is a Tswana population of 1,700,000 in the Republic of South Africa and the Tswana of Botswana are therefore far outnumbered by the Tswana of the Republic. The latter mainly occupy an arc extending southwards from the western Transvaal round into the country south of the Molopo, the northern extremity of the Cape Province of South Africa. They live in well-defined areas in a land where their ancestors originally settled and where, before the coming of the Europeans, the Tswana could roam more or less at will. Against this background Kgabo's little migration, a commonplace in Tswana history, has considerable significance. By leading his people a few miles to the west he not only secured an independent chiefship for himself but he also sowed the first seed of an independent nation.

Unlike most African peoples, who live scattered in homesteads and small villages, the Tswana live in towns. The practice is an ancient one. It was well established at the beginning of the nineteenth century and had no doubt been the custom long before then, perhaps going back to the origins of the tribe.

When Trüter and Somerville visited Dithakong in 1801 the Tlhaping were in fact sharing the town with a dissident group of Rolong. Later the two tribes separated and in 1812 Burchell thought that the then capital of the Tlhaping, which was on another site but was still called Dithakong, held five thousand people, though he concedes that there may have been more. Modern Tswana towns are considerably larger. Serowe, principal town of the Ngwato, has a population of 43,000, while Kanye, capital of the Ngwaketse, has 39,000 inhabitants. The population of Gaborone is 18,000 but this figure is due to the emergence of that town as capital of Botswana and does not represent a natural growth.*

Besides the principal town of the tribe, where the chief lives with the ruling community around him, there are also in most areas subsidiary but still important settlements. These are generally but not always occupied by the affiliated tribes. One of many examples is Shoshong, once the capital of the Ngwato, where the population is now composed of Kaa and Phaleng.

A Tswana town is really a collection of small villages, each village being the habitat of a ward; and a ward is 'a collection of households living together in their own hamlet, and forming a distinct social and political unit under the leadership and authority of an hereditary headman'.[15] The observant Burchell noticed this at Dithakong. 'In our way', he wrote, 'we passed through many *clusters of houses*; between which there were most frequently large spaces of unoccupied ground. Each of these clusters might generally be considered as the village of a different *kósi* or chieftain, and inhabited for the greater part, by his relations and connections; yet not necessarily, nor perhaps always, following this as a rule.'[16]

The dominant feature of each town is the *kgotla*. This is a crescent-shaped windbreak of poles, where the men meet to

---

* The figures are taken from the 1971 census and are rounded to the nearest thousand. The population of Gaborone has probably continued to grow disproportionately since the census was taken.

discuss their affairs. Each village, and in the towns each ward, has its *kgotla*, the most important being the *kgotla* of the chief's own ward. It is here that the daily business of the tribe is carried out.

In the past the Tswana often abandoned their well-built towns to migrate elsewhere. The cause might be war, political dissension, drought, famine, or simply a deterioration in local conditions. The Tlhaping moved four times between 1802 and 1817. More recently the Ngwato, who had gone from Shoshong to 'old' Palapye in 1889, moved again in 1902 to a new capital at Serowe. Under more settled political conditions, with the development of better water facilities and the establishment in towns of permanent institutions like hospitals and schools, such upheavals have not occurred for a long time.

Chiefship among the Tswana is hereditary, usually passing from father to son, and the position was always one of great prestige and authority. 'The king of the Beetjuans', wrote Lichtenstein, 'has nearly uncircumscribed power, since he can punish all offences according to his own pleasure, and no one has any right to oppose his decisions.'[17] This is certainly an exaggeration, but it remains true that the chief was the central figure of tribal government, 'at once ruler, judge, maker and guardian of the law, repository of wealth, dispenser of gifts, leader in war, priest and magician of the people'. His duties, if he carried them out faithfully, could impose an immense burden on his time and energy. His work might indeed be more than he was able successfully to cope with, since owing to his 'pivotal position' in the life of the tribe, nothing could be done without his support and co-operation.[18]

The chief was not left to shoulder his heavy task alone but was surrounded by a widening circle of advisory councils. First there was an intimate body of confidential advisers, usually senior relatives, whom he consulted privately and informally on matters of tribal administration. Outside this inner council there was a more formal body consisting of headmen, who were specially summoned to discuss matters of urgency and importance. Finally there was an assembly of the men of the whole tribe, which met to discuss matters of public concern and was called together by the chief whenever the occasion arose.

Although the Tswana always held the chief and the institution of chiefship in special reverence, these councils, besides helping the chief to govern, placed effective restraints on his power. No chief, if he was wise, would act against the advice of his councillors or without their support. The oft-quoted Tswana saying, *Kgosi ke kgosi ka morafe*, a chief is chief by grace of the tribe, was generally valid, and in comparatively recent times several chiefs have lost their positions, and one his life, for forgetting it.

Time and its changes have mercilessly eroded the position of the chief. The introduction of European rule limited his administrative and judicial functions and put a stop to the wars in which he might lead the tribe. With the coming of Christianity his religious and magical activities largely ceased. More destructive still has been the impact of even later developments: the growth of political parties which cut across tribal bonds and transfer popular loyalty from the chief to other personalities; the establishment of district councils, which have virtually taken over the chiefs' role in local government; election of commoners to the legislature, which creates a new centre of power that may be inimical to the aristocratic principle; the constitution itself, which by relegating the chiefs to a relatively impotent second chamber, denies them a decisive voice in territorial affairs. It remains to be seen whether the chiefship will survive at all, or whether, like the Indian princes, the chiefs will remain generally respected figures but in all important matters ineffectual except in so far as they can, as individuals, capture a place in the new set-up by force of personality.*

---

* For more about this see pp. 182–4.

The economy of the Tswana will be described in a later chapter but it is appropriate to mention here that the habit of living in towns is the reason for an unusual kind of land distribution. Land and grazing near the towns soon become exhausted, and the people are therefore compelled to push further and further afield. Thus was evolved the system of lands and cattle posts, belonging to the town but at a distance from it. A man may have his land twenty or thirty miles from the town in one direction and his cattle post as far or much further in the other. The lands are located in blocks or zones within which many families may have their fields side by side or close together. These areas are used exclusively for cultivation, and no one may live permanently in them or have cattle posts there. The cattle post, which is sited with particular attention to water and grazing, consists of thornbuilt enclosures, large and small, and perhaps a few crude huts, the whole surrounded by an area of pasture. The cattle post is frequently in the charge of an employee, and the herdsboys are often the owner's own small sons.

As may be imagined, the prosecution of these wide-scattered interests involves the Tswana in a great deal of travelling. From October or November until May, and even later in the north, ploughing, sowing and harvest demand the presence on the lands of at least some members of the family, though not necessarily of the head. During these times the towns are almost deserted, the whole of the population, with all its movable property, having migrated to the lands. Meanwhile the head of the family, or his grown-up sons, must visit the cattle posts – he may have more than one – and this involves an absence of several weeks. Altogether it may be said that the ordinary Tswana hardly spends four or five months of the year in the town, while the rest is spent at the cattle post or on his land. But the town always remains the base for the individual, as well as the hub of tribal life.

II · The Missionaries

'At three, P.M. [sic] reaching the summit of the hill, Lattakoo came all at once into view, lying in a valley between hills, stretching about three or four miles from E. to W.'[1]

Our traveller was a very different personality from the administrators and explorers who had hitherto visited the Tlhaping. This was the Reverend John Campbell, sent out to South Africa by the London Missionary Society in 1812 'to visit the country, personally to inspect the different [missionary] settlements, and to establish such regulations . . . as might be most conducive to the attainment of the great end proposed – the conversion of the heathen, keeping in view at the same time the promotion of their civilization'.[2] He was also to select sites for new centres of work.

Campbell certainly did not skimp his task. Travelling by ox-wagon he went first to Bethelsdorp five hundred miles east of Cape Town, then north over the boundary of the Colony and across the Orange river to Dithakong, where he arrived in June 1813; from there into Namaqualand, and thence back to Cape Town down the west coast.

There was now a new chief of the Tlhaping. Molehabangwe had died a few months before Burchell's visit in 1812 and his son Mothibi reigned in his stead. John Campbell, who was accompanied to Dithakong by the missionaries James Read from Bethelsdorp and William Anderson from Griqualand, lost no time in broaching the object of his visit. It was, he said, to ask for the chief's permission to send teachers to the Tlhaping, and for Mothibi's protection when they came. Mothibi made surprisingly little demur and after a short debate came out with the historic invitation, which Campbell prints in capital letters,

'SEND INSTRUCTORS, AND I WILL BE A FATHER TO THEM'. So were laid the foundations of the London Missionary Society's station at Kuruman, which was to become the best-known, though for some years the most remote, English Protestant mission in southern Africa.

The London Missionary Society answered Mothibi's invitation in 1815, when John Evans and Robert Hamilton were sent to Dithakong to open the new mission, arriving there early in 1816. 'They came', writes Robert Moffat, 'with the most sanguine hopes of a hearty welcome from the proffered paternal care of Mothibi', but the reality was very different. From Moffat's narrative it is possible to deduce that the Tlhaping, although they had remained silent at the time, disliked Mothibi's invitation to Campbell and had taken the chief to task for it. This time their feelings towards the visitors were not in doubt. 'The missionaries must not come here', they shouted; and as Evans and Hamilton sadly prepared to leave, 'the barbarous people followed these rejected heralds of salvation . . . with hooting and derisive vociferations'.[3] A second attempt was no more successful and it was left to the experienced James Read, who arrived in Dithakong at the end of 1816, to secure a foothold in Mothibi's country. Read not only obtained permission to remain, but he also persuaded the chief to move the tribal capital to the Kuruman river. The move took place in June 1817, shortly after the disastrous failure of an expedition led by Mothibi against the Kwena, in which the chief himself was wounded and narrowly escaped with his life. The new capital was at first called 'New Lattakoo', but it soon became known as Kuruman.

The Kuruman river, like so many rivers in this region, is generally dry throughout most of its length, but it has a remarkable source. This is the spring or 'eye' of Kuruman, called by the Tswana, Gasegonyane, where a veritable underground river bursts into the open, delivering a volume of water of four to five million gallons a day. 'It not only gushed from a cavern of rocks as from the sluice of a mill-dam', reported Trüter, 'but in innumerable springs spouted up out of an extensive bed of white crystallized pebbles and quartzose sand, forming, at not more than a hundred paces from its source, a stream of at least thirty feet wide and two feet deep, called the *Kourmanna* or *Booshuana* river, whose direction was to the northward.'[4]

The arrival of the missionaries established a permanent connection between the southern Tswana and Europeans. Comparing these newcomers with the travellers who had preceded them, the Tlhaping probably found the experience surprising. The missionaries were by definition dedicated evangelists, and in the spirit of the time not at all disposed to find virtues in heathen life and society. The Tlhaping were no longer 'this friendly and hospitable people' (Trüter), their attitude to clothing 'extremely modest' (Lichtenstein), their way of life worthy, as Burchell thought, of detailed investigation and description. They now became ignorant savages, to be pitied not applauded, with unedifying customs and ceremonies that were 'prodigious barriers to the Gospel' (Robert Moffat). Even to Livingstone, who was generally less intolerant than some of his colleagues, the Tswana were 'sunk into the very lowest state of both mental and moral degradation' and their depravity was 'subnatural'.[5]

Neither by instinct nor training were the missionaries qualified to recognize that the people of the vast field that opened before them had a well developed religious system of their own. 'The dominant cult', says Schapera,

was the worship of ancestral spirits (*badimo*). Each family was held to be under the supernatural guidance and protection of its deceased ancestors in the male line, to whom sacrifices were offered and prayers said on all occasions of domestic importance. The head of the family acted as priest, a role that gave him considerable authority over his dependants. The people also believed in a high God, named *Modimo*, who was regarded as the creator of all things and the moulder of destiny. He was vaguely associated with the phenomena of the weather, and punished innovations, or departure from established usage, by sending wind, hail, or heat, and withholding the rain; and death, if not attributable to sorcery, was spoken of as 'an act of God'. He was, however, considered too remote from the world of man to be directly approached, and prayers or sacrifices were seldom offered to him, although at times the ancestral spirits might be implored to intercede with him.[6]

These were the beliefs that the missionaries, if they apprehended them at all, set out to combat and replace with the truth as it had been revealed to them.*

Read, together with Hamilton, worked at Kuruman until 1820, when Read was removed and sent to Bethelsdorp, leaving Hamilton to struggle on with a Griqua assistant and a few Hottentots. This unsatisfactory situation lasted until the following year when there arrived one who was to make of Kuruman not only an active centre of Christian civilization but also a symbol to people in England of missionary effort in southern Africa, and a springboard for the evangelization of the region lying to the north.

Like several others of the Society's famous missionaries, Robert Moffat was a Scotsman. He was born of humble parents at Ormiston in 1795, and after the normal Scottish elementary education, supplemented by the teaching of his sternly pious but kindly mother, he became a gardener's apprentice at the age of fourteen. He underwent an intense

* One day Campbell, inspired by the majestic solitude of the country around him, gave expression to his feelings in fervent doggerel. In these regions where no white men come, he says, the people have never heard the Gospel:

> Indeed they know not that there's one
> Ruling on high, and GOD alone.

But this is precisely what the Tswana *did* know.

religious experience not uncommon among young people at that time, and at the age of twenty he resolved to 'get landed on some island or foreign shore, where I might teach poor heathen to know the Saviour'.[7]

At Dukinfield near Manchester, Moffat worked for a time in the nursery gardens of James Smith, a Scotsman who had changed his name from Gow on coming to England. Here Moffat fell in love with Smith's daughter Mary, in whom he found a 'warm missionary heart'. But Smith was reluctant to part with his daughter at once, and when Moffat was accepted by the London Missionary Society and sailed for South Africa in 1816, he travelled alone.

There followed several years of travel and adventure in the Cape and in Namaqualand, and it was not until 1821 that Moffat took up permanent residence at Kuruman. With him was Mary, who had come to South Africa to marry him in 1819, and their new-born daughter, also Mary, who was destined to become the wife of David Livingstone.

Moffat was a man of extraordinary zeal, perseverance and courage, but of all the missionaries of the Society he was the least sympathetic towards African culture. This, to him, was a mere hotchpotch of ridiculous and harmful superstitions. As to African religion, it did not exist: 'He [Satan] has employed his agency, with fatal success, in erasing every vestige of religious impression from the minds of the Bechuanas, Hottentots, and Bushmen; leaving them without a single ray to guide them from the dark and dread futurity, or a single link to unite them with the skies.'[8] Moffat had really no interest in Africans as personalities, but only as objects of conversion to his view of Christianity.

His uncompromising outlook extended to his fellow-missionaries. The missionary, he held, had only one important task. This was to spread the Gospel among the heathen. He therefore disapproved of those who, like the great John Philip, regarded it as their duty also to champion the cause of oppressed African

peoples. It is only fair to note that Moffat at Kuruman, unlike
Philip and his colleagues at the Cape, had not always under his
eyes the injustices which the Hottentots suffered at the hands
of the white colonists.

The first years at Kuruman were strenuous and unrewarding.
Moffat's gardener's eye immediately perceived the potentialities
of the Kuruman river as a means of irrigation, and he persuaded the chief to move the tribal capital further up-river
towards the source, to Seoding, where the mission stands now.
Helped by the faithful Hamilton, Moffat spent his energies in
endless exertion. The missionaries turned their hands to carpentry, smithing and brick-making. They built houses and a
church, dug a trench three miles long to lead water from the
Kuruman source, made gardens, planted trees and vines. 'With
very great labour,' wrote John Philip, 'the missionaries have
succeeded in erecting a neat row of houses in the bottom of the
valley; to each house is attached a large garden, enclosed with a
neat fence. The gardens have been laid out, by Mr Moffat, with
much taste; and, from his knowledge of horticulture, they have
been stocked with a variety of seeds and edible roots. In front
of the houses, and at a distance of, perhaps, forty feet, is the
canal by which the water has been led out from the river.' [9]

These peaceful if arduous pursuits were conducted in an
atmosphere of tension and anxiety. This was the time of the
difaqane, when the wars of the Zulu chief Shaka had thrown
southern Africa into chaos. The backwash lapped distant
Bechuanaland, where in 1823 a savage horde, part-refugees part-
banditti, occupied the old Tlhaping capital Dithakong. The
threat to Kuruman was acute, but it was averted by Robert
Moffat, who went quickly to Griquatown, where he enlisted the
help of Melvill, the Government agent, and a troop of Griqua
mounted riflemen, and with them rode to Dithakong. The
occupants fiercely resisted attempts to bring them to parley and
sallied out to attack. The starving horde fought with desperate
courage but was no match for men with rifles and was soon put

to flight. Moffat and Melvill were able at some personal risk to rescue numbers of women and children from the vengeful Tlhaping.

Although the immediate danger was past, the following years were difficult and depressing. The people remained deaf to the missionaries' teaching; bands of marauders roamed the country-side and sometimes threatened the mission; there was a long drought and then swarms of locusts descended on the valley and ate every scrap of vegetation; Mothibi drifted away from Kuruman with most of his people. In spite of these setbacks the missionaries refused to be discouraged and their patience was in time rewarded. By 1828 the threat to the security of the mission from hostile tribes had disappeared, and in 1829 the first converts were baptized.

The year 1829 was noteworthy for yet another reason. In the latter part of the year, Kuruman received some interesting visitors. They were envoys from Mzilikazi, chief of the Mata-bele, whose curiosity had been aroused by tales about the white men. Suitably impressed by what they saw, the envoys pre-pared to leave but Moffat, fearing that they might be murdered by the people along the road, escorted them back to the town of their chief, which was then near the site of modern Pretoria.

The Matabele were not native to this region. When Shaka, at the beginning of his career, smashed his rivals the Ndwandwe, several of the defeated chieftains moved beyond his reach. Soshangane fled up the east coast to Portuguese East Africa, where he founded the tribe now called Shangaan. Zwangendaba took his people even further afield, and their descendants are the Ngoni in the south of Tanzania, east of Lake Malawi. Mzilikazi, however, submitted to the victor and served him for a while. Then, after a successful campaign, he appropriated the booty himself instead of taking it back to his master, turned freebooter on his own account and withdrew to the Transvaal. The Matabele, who were trained in Zulu warfare and governed with the same ferocious discipline, spread death and destruction among the tribes around them.

With Moffat's visit to Mzilikazi in 1829 there began one of the strangest friendships that have united two men. The barbaric chief conceived an extraordinary devotion for the stern, uncompromising missionary, a devotion that remained undiminished for more than thirty years, though the two were only to come together five times, at long intervals. Moffat could not understand Mzilikazi's affection for him. It even to some extent disturbed him, but he appreciated the influence it gave him over the chief. He used it to induce the chief to mitigate the severity of his justice, and to make concessions to a degree that was almost dangerous to himself in a society accustomed to cruelty as a means of enforcing the law. Although there was no possibility that Mzilikazi, with all his overflowing goodwill, would allow himself to be converted to Christianity, Moffat was able to obtain permission to establish a mission station in Matabeleland.

The friendship of Moffat and Mzilikazi was to exercise a fateful influence in the next generation, when John Smith Moffat, the son of Robert, negotiated the Moffat Treaty with Mzilikazi's son Lobengula. Meanwhile other actors entered the Tswana scene. These were the Boers, who by the late 'thirties had arrived in the Magaliesberg.

III · The Great Trek — Livingstone — The Tswana at Mid-century

The Great Trek of the Boers from the Cape Colony to the interior is the central event of modern South African history, and it has received correspondingly thorough treatment from historians.[1] At the risk of repeating things that have often been said elsewhere, it is necessary to make something more than a passing reference to it here, since the effects of the Trek, both immediate and remote, were a vital element in the history of the Tswana during the nineteenth century.

The mainly Dutch-descended frontier farmers of the Cape Colony, known as Boers, were a remarkable people by any standards. Necessity and instinct made them semi-nomadic pastoralists, whose wealth lay in their cattle and their sheep. Living as they did in small patriarchal groups in the vast expanses of the interior they had developed a character and a specialized way of life adapted to the environment. They were independent to a fault, proud, brave and self-reliant, tenacious and enduring. They were good riders and fine shots, depending for food on the game which fell to their guns, turning the skins into clothes and shoes, and trading with Hottentots and peddlers for the few necessities that they could not supply themselves. In hardiness and courage the women matched the men.

These admirable qualities had their reverse side. Their isolation had left the Boers in darkest ignorance of everything outside their own narrow world. 'For want of formal education and sufficient pastors, they read their Bibles intensively, drawing from the Old Testament, which spoke the authentic language of their lives, a justification of themselves, of their beliefs and their habits. Continued immigration, even of such small groups as the

French Huguenots, would have done much to keep them abreast
of some of the thought of the new Europe of the Enlightenment.
Instead the remotest corner of Europe was better informed.'[2]
Above all the Boers held as an article of faith that between
themselves and the native peoples with whom they were in
contact, there was a great gulf fixed. They utterly rejected any
suggestion that there could be any sort of equality between
good Christian men and people like the Hottentots or the Bantu
of the eastern frontier. Economically brown men and black men
had their uses as servants and labourers. Otherwise they were
totally outside the scope of white society. The doctrine of
apartheid has a long history.

The Boers had an inexhaustible appetite for land, and land of
sorts was to all appearance inexhaustible. The pastoralists of
the dry interior required far larger areas for their cattle than the
coastal belt farmers needed to grow their crops. The frontiers-
man was raised in the firm tradition that his birthright was a
farm of 6000 acres or more, very roughly measured, occupied
at a tiny rent on conditions that almost amounted to freehold.*

A Boer's chief possessions were his oxen and his wagons, his
horses and his guns. Without these the life he led would have
been impossible. Houses were of various kinds. Some were comfortable and roomy, others were simple constructions of clay
and thatch, yet others flimsy shelters of reeds. Many Boers used
their wagons as houses for a great part of the year. Attached to
the family as servants and labourers were Hottentots and
slaves.[3]

The Boers had their own form of law and government. Cape
Town was too remote to make much impact on them, and what
they knew of the central Government they did not like. 'Long
before the [Dutch East India] Company's day was done, the
Boers had decided that the business of a central government

---

* This was the 'loan-place' system. The rent was about £5 annually for
6000 acres, and as long as the tenant paid the rent he had complete
security. He could even sell his farm or bequeath it.

was to appoint suitable local officials, to supply the outlying districts with ammunition, and to defend the coasts of the Colony from invaders. For the rest it should leave men alone.'[4] The local officials were the *landdrost*, an administrator with judicial powers; the *heemraden*, who sat with the *landdrost* as assessors in hearing cases and dealing with the affairs of the community; and field cornets, officials whose duties were originally military but who later acquired functions resembling those of a justice of the peace.

In 1806 the British occupied Cape Town for the second time, and this time they came to stay. The event brought great changes to the South African scene. The new Government showed that it was determined to govern, and in its own way. The old system of land tenure was done away with and a more economical and less casual one substituted; the administration of justice was reformed and the courts made accessible to Hottentots as well as to Europeans; the currency was stabilized and the economy stimulated. British immigrants driven from the mother country by unemployment after the Napoleonic Wars demanded and obtained various civic rights and liberties. Most fateful of all, the gates were opened to a flood of liberal and humanitarian ideas from which South Africa had hitherto been insulated. British rule brought with it the abolition of slavery and a totally new concept of the relationship between black and white.

To the Boers these changes appeared to threaten the very bases of their free, unhurried, spacious way of life. They disliked the new land settlement which curtailed their holdings; they distrusted the British attitude towards the problems of the eastern frontier, where the Bantu were pushing south as the Europeans pushed north; most of all the Boers resented the establishment of political equality between black and white and the refusal of the British Government to maintain 'proper relations between master and servant'.

About 1835 all these grievances, combined with the naturally nomadic tendencies of the frontiersmen, culminated in the Trek. This migratory process lasted for some thirteen years, and although the number of people involved was small (an estimated 14,000 during the first decade), the political and social results for South Africa can hardly be overstated.[5] As far as the Tswana are concerned, the effect was to bring the trekkers up to the very borders of their country. After defeating the Matabele at Mosega in 1837, Boers under A. H. Potgieter settled in the Magaliesberg, where they were hailed by the local tribes as liberators. Worried at the same time by the threatening proximity of Zulu *impis*, Mzilikazi withdrew to the north, to found the capital of a new empire in the country that came to be called Matabeleland. The Boers now saw themselves as successors by conquest to all Mzilikazi's former domains. These they took to be a very large slice indeed of south-central Africa, far larger than that over which the Matabele had held effective sway.

While these events were taking place in the Cape Colony, the mission at Kuruman made steady growth under the care of Robert Moffat, ably seconded by Hamilton. But it was still the northernmost outpost of the Society and about 1840 it was decided to take an important step forward. When therefore David Livingstone, having joined the Society in 1838, arrived in South Africa in 1841, he was under instructions to turn his attention to the region north of Kuruman. Between 1841 and 1843 he made four extended tours to the interior before settling at Mabotsa in the western Transvaal about thirty miles north of Zeerust, among a group of Kgatla under a chief named Mosielele. There he had a desperate encounter with a lion that might have cost him his life, and during his convalescence at Kuruman he married Mary, the daughter of Robert Moffat.

Livingstone was not one to work easily in double harness, and having quarrelled with Rogers Edwards, his colleague at Mabotsa, he moved further north to attach himself to the Kwena of chief Setshele, who were then at Tshonwane. In 1847 he persuaded the chief to take the tribe to the Kolobeng river in modern Botswana, and there Livingstone built his new station, the ruins of which can still be seen, about fifteen miles west of Gaborone.

Trouble soon blew up between missionary and chief on the one hand and the voortrekkers in the western Transvaal on the other. The Boers had no love for missionaries, least of all for those of the London Missionary Society. Was it not John Philip, superintendent of the Society in Cape Town, who led the humanitarian attack on the treatment of Hottentots in the Colony? Was it not the same John Philip who had procured the passage of the 50th Ordinance of 1828 which removed discriminatory enactments against the Hottentots, with the result, according to the Boers, that the Hottentots became lawless vagrants? And were not the missionaries, especially those of the London Missionary Society, foremost in destroying those 'proper relations between master and servant' on which society and the economy rested?

Against Livingstone the Boers had a special grievance. They believed that he supplied firearms to the Kwena, and this to them was a very grave offence indeed. In the course of their wanderings and in their battles with adversaries who outnumbered them many times, the trekkers owed their victories and often their lives to their skill with the rifle and their monopoly of its possession. They were haunted by the fear that this weapon, with which a few determined men and women could drive off many hundreds of fierce adversaries armed with spears, might fall into the hands of hostile tribesmen. There was no subject on which the Boers were more sensitive.

The Boers had another reason for disliking Setshele. His country straddled the 'missionaries' road', the track leading north from Kuruman to Shoshong, whence other roads ran on into central Africa. The 'missionaries' road' was thus the highway to the country beyond the Transvaal, and whoever controlled it also controlled access to the interior. Setshele's chief fault in the eyes of the Boers, according to Livingstone, lay in his hospitality to British missionaries and traders, in whom they saw the spearhead of a British advance to the north. This they correctly believed would be a barrier to their own expansion.

Indeed to many trekkers the result of the Trek had proved in some sort illusory. They had expected to find in the interior unlimited new territory that they could make their own. But the emptiness that had impressed the first trekkers was temporary and artificial. It had been caused by the wars of Shaka the Zulu and their consequences, and when peace was restored there was no lack of claimants to the open spaces. In addition the Boers found themselves surrounded on the fringe of the lands that they occupied by tribes that had managed to remain unsubdued. To the north and west of the Magaliesberg there was a strong belt of Tswana over whom the London Missionary Society was gaining influence. Extremely sensitive to the proximity of powerful independent chiefs, the Boers regarded Setshele as ambitious and aggressive, a dangerous man to have on their western border, especially as he appeared to be well provided with firearms.

Livingstone vigorously repudiated the allegations of gun-running, pouring scorn on his accusers' credulity, and counter-attacked with charges of slavery on the part of the farmers. One aspect of their labour system was particularly controversial. It was called apprenticeship. This had originated in the need to find useful work for the idle and the destitute, and consisted in placing people of this kind to work for farmers, with guarantees on either side. But abuses crept in. Among the apprentices were 'orphans' picked up by the Boers in raids and reprisals on the native tribes. The suspicion grew that raids were undertaken for the sole purpose of manufacturing orphans to supplement a deficient labour supply. Even if allegations of slavery were exaggerated, there was plenty of evidence of forced unpaid labour. 'I have myself', wrote Livingstone, 'been an eye-witness of Boers coming to a village, and, according to their usual custom, demanding twenty or thirty women to weed their gardens, and have seen these women proceed to the scene of un-requited toil, carrying their own food on their heads, their children on their backs, and instruments of labour on their shoulders.' [6]

Differences between missionary, chief and farmers came to a head in 1852 when a Boer commando raided Setshele's town of Dimawe, dispersed the defenders and took a large number of women and children as prisoners. In the course of the raid Livingstone's mission at Kolobeng was ransacked and de-stroyed.[7]

Setshele's complaints and those of the London Missionary Society failed to extract from the Colonial Secretary in London more than an instruction to the High Commissioner to check such 'unjustifiable proceedings'. To this was added a warning that the High Commissioner must not go beyond 'friendly remonstrances' to those in authority over the peccant Boers. For this was the year of the Sand River Convention, when the British Government, through Commissioners Hogge and Owen, guaranteed to the Transvaal Boers 'the right to manage their own affairs and to govern themselves according to their own laws, without any interference on the part of the British Government'. One clause of the Convention that was to prove especially damaging to the African inhabitants was that which prevented them from buying ammunition while specifically allowing the Boers to do so freely. In 1854 came the Bloem-fontein Convention, whereby Great Britain abandoned the Orange River Sovereignty. In that climate there was clearly no prospect of serious British intervention on behalf of a Scottish missionary and an African chief.

While he was based on Kolobeng Livingstone began those explorations that were to make his name a household word. Lake Ngami had been known by reputation to the Kwena for many years. To Livingstone it was an irresistible lure, and in June 1849, accompanied by William Cotton Oswell and Mungo

Murray, he set out to find the lake. The party turned north-west before reaching Shoshong, and struck the Boteti river at its north-easterly bend. They followed the Boteti westwards, meeting the Yei, then as now an important tribe of Ngamiland. They then came to the Thamalakane, and on 1 August 1849 Lake Ngami, 'this fine-looking sheet of water', was seen by Europeans for the first time. The lake was shallow, and the process of desiccation, which is now complete, was already noticeable.

Livingstone had hoped from Lake Ngami to visit Sebetwane, chief of the Kololo tribe in the Zambezi valley, but Letshola-thebe, chief of the Tawana of Ngamiland, who was on bad terms with Sebetwane, obstructed the plan because, says Livingstone, he was afraid that the expedition would open the way to traders who would supply his enemy with guns. So there was nothing for it but to return to Kolobeng. Another attempt in the following year, this time by the whole Living-stone family accompanied by Setshele, was no more successful, and it was not until 1851 that Livingstone, again with his wife and children and this time with Oswell, succeeded in reaching Sebetwane at his capital on the Chobe river.

This chief was head of the Patsa, a section of the Fokeng, a tribe of Sotho origin which, like so many other tribes, had been driven from its home during the confusion of the *difaqane*. Sebetwane led his people from their home in the present Orange Free State northwards through Bechuanaland then by a circu-itous route through the Lake Ngami region and the Okavango swamps till he came to the Zambezi valley, some 800 miles from where he started. The Kololo, as Sebetwane's people were now called, subdued the local tribes and founded an extensive em-pire that stretched up towards the Kafue, westwards into Barotseland and south as far as the Chobe.

Sebetwane welcomed the missionaries and promised to help Livingstone find a site for a new station. But he fell ill and died while the Livingstones were still in his town, to Livingstone's great sorrow. He was succeeded in the chiefship by his daughter Mmamotshisane from whom Livingstone obtained permission to explore the country, and he and Oswell, travelling one hundred and thirty miles north-east from the Chobe, discovered the Zambezi river at Sesheke at the end of June 1851.

Convinced that 'there was no hope of the Boers allowing the peaceable instruction of the natives at Kolobeng', and resolved to look for a site for a station in the new field that was now open to him, Livingstone decided to send his family to England so as not to expose them to the perils of the climate. He put them on board a ship at Cape Town and it was on his return to Kuruman that he heard about the Boer raid on Dimawe.

From this point Livingstone disappears from our story. He set off again for the Zambezi in 1853, and this was the beginning of the prodigious journey which took him to Loanda on the west coast and back across Africa to Quielimane on the Indian Ocean. He did not return to the Tswana again.

The Boer fear of British rivalry in the interior was not unjustified. Moving about the region between the Limpopo and Ngamiland there were at this time a number of British traders and hunters to whom the country offered fine opportunities for profit and sport. Among the earliest of the traders was David Hume (1796–1863) who travelled extensively among the Ngwato in the 'thirties. He accompanied Robert Moffat and Dr Andrew Smith when they visited Mzilikazi near Zeerust in 1835. James Chapman (1831–72) was at once trader, explorer, photographer and naturalist. He was a good friend of the missionaries, a sympathetic observer of local customs and he wrote a classic of African travel. Samuel Edwards, 'Far Interior Sam' (1827–1922), the best-known of the trader-pioneers, was son of the missionary colleague with whom Livingstone quarrelled at Mabotsa. Edwards began hunting and trading in Bechuanaland in 1848 and in the course of a long life took part in many important events in Bechuanaland and Matabeleland. J. H.

Wilson, active between 1840 and 1870, married a daughter of Setshele and claimed to have seen Lake Ngami before Livingstone. Joseph McCabe (1816–70), trader and botanical collector, crossed the Kgalagadi in 1852. One would like to include George Westbeech (?–1888), a popular and influential trader in the Zambezi valley, though his business had more to do with Barotseland than with Bechuanaland. The most notable of the 'sportsmen' were R. G. Gordon Cumming (1820–66) and W. C. Baldwin (1830–1903). Of the two Baldwin was the more bloodthirsty. Both left accounts of their destructive exploits.

From the records of missionaries, traders and travellers it is possible to form a picture of Bechuanaland as it was in the middle of the nineteenth century.[8] During the 'twenties and 'thirties the Tswana had endured the backwash of the *difaqane* and for them the period was one of defeat and dispersion. The Tlhaping, as we have seen, barely escaped invasion, while the tribes north of them fell successively to Sebetwane's Kololo as these made their fighting march to the Zambezi. After the Kololo came the Matabele as Mzilikazi migrated to the north away from the Magaliesberg Boers.

Still the Tswana made a surprising recovery. By the 'fifties and 'sixties the major tribes were back in or near their old homes in roughly the same areas in which we find them today. On the frontiers the Matabele and the Boers were still a menace (in the case of the latter a growing one), while there remained many inter-tribal and dynastic disputes and differences. But compared with the situation as it was twenty or thirty years earlier the impression among the more northerly tribes at any rate, those of modern Botswana, is one of increasing stability.

The Kwena, after their troubles with the Boers, had moved to a more secure position at Dithubaruba in the Dithejwane hills. Their chief, Setshele, had been Livingstone's first convert, having taken the plunge in 1848. As a prior condition to admission to the Church, he had been required to send away his plural wives and this had caused some stir in the tribe. Although

Livingstone abandoned him in 1853 after a ministry punctuated by long absences, the chief stayed faithful after his fashion. The Kwena were without a missionary for several years until the Hermannsburg Mission, which was German Lutheran, sent men to work with the tribe. In 1866, however, after the Hermannsburg missionaries had left, the London Missionary Society again started work among the Kwena.

The Ngwato were living at Shoshong under chief Sekgoma, who had ruled the tribe through troubled times and had brought them back to their ancient capital after some years of dispersion. Here they enjoyed a short period of tranquillity which was brought to an end by the interference of chief Setshele in the affairs of the tribe.

Setshele had spent much of his troubled and adventurous youth among the Ngwato, and he had married Mokgokong, a daughter of the Ngwato chief Kgari. Throughout his life he maintained a close interest in Ngwato affairs, in which he meddled industriously and in the event disastrously. When Robert Moffat passed through the Kwena country in 1854 on his way to visit Mzilikazi, Setshele besought him to bring Matsheng, rightful heir to the Ngwato chiefship, back from the Matabele. Although Moffat did nothing about Setshele's request on this occasion, he brought Matsheng back on a subsequent visit, with unfortunate results for the Ngwato and for Matsheng himself.

Matsheng derived his title from a peculiarity of Tswana law. Chief Kgari, who was killed in a tribal war about 1826, had three wives about whom we know. The chief wife Mmapolao was childless; the second, Bobjwale, had a son named Khama, and the third, Dibeelane, a son named Sekgoma. When Kgari was killed, his cousin Sedimo, regent during Khama's minority, 'entered the hut' of Bobjwale to 'raise seed' to the dead man, and she in due course bore a son. By the law of the levirate, to which the Ngwato subscribe, this child was in the direct line to the chiefship after Khama, since his mother was the senior childbearing wife of the dead chief. Who the actual father was did not matter.

Khama duly succeeded Kgari and died after a short reign. His half-brother Sekgoma then assumed the chiefship but not before he had quarrelled violently with Bobjwale, who fled with the boy Matsheng to take refuge with the Kwena. Here Matsheng was taken prisoner by a party of Matabele, and grew up as a warrior of Mzilikazi. Meanwhile Sekgoma continued to rule the Ngwato.

The arrival of Matsheng from Matabeleland and his installation as chief marked the beginning of an era of chronic unrest among the Ngwato. Two intertwining threads are discernible in the confusion. The first was misrule on the part of the new chief, who as a result was twice compelled to flee the country and ended his days in exile. The other was the rift between Sekgoma, a staunch upholder of ancient customs and beliefs, and his resolutely Christian son Khama. Another son, Kgamane, was also a Christian and was likewise an object of his father's anger. (He eventually turned against Khama and aligned himself with Sekgoma.) These conflicts, which the machinations of Setshele did nothing to assuage, did not come to an end until the definitive installation of Khama as chief in 1875.

Sekgoma had a bad press all his life especially from the missionaries. This was because of his determined heathenism and his quarrels with Khama, whom the missionaries regarded as the exemplar of an African Christian. Sekgoma did not deserve his bad reputation, and unflattering descriptions of him by contemporary Europeans should be discounted. He was tough, resolute, clever, well versed in tribal law and in all the functions of chiefship. In his own place and time he was a conspicuously able leader, and so the Ngwato in retrospect justly regard him.

The third of the northern tribes, the Ngwaketse, were hammered successively by the Mantatees,* the Kololo and the

---

* These were a horde of Tlokwa thrown up by the *difaqane*. They were led by a chieftainess named Mmantatisi and her son Sekonyela.

Matabele. They were dispersed in several small groups in places as far apart as the western Kgalagadi and Taung near the Harts river. By the middle 'fifties, however, these fragments had come together under chief Gaseitsiwe round Kanye, the present

THE NGWATO SUCCESSION

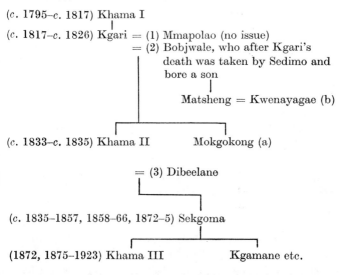

(c. 1795–c. 1817) Khama I

(c. 1817–c. 1826) Kgari = (1) Mmapolao (no issue)
= (2) Bobjwale, who after Kgari's death was taken by Sedimo and bore a son

Matsheng = Kwenayagae (b)

(c. 1833–c. 1835) Khama II   Mokgokong (a)

= (3) Dibeelane

(c. 1835–1857, 1858–66, 1872–5) Sekgoma

(1872, 1875–1923) Khama III   Kgamane etc.

(a) became the wife of Setshele and was sent away by him with other plural wives when he became a Christian.
(b) became the wife of Setshele in his old age after the death of Matsheng.

tribal capital. About this time the London Missionary Society sent an African pastor to labour among them, and with the accession of Gaseitsiwe traders began to settle in Kanye.

When Livingstone first saw Lake Ngami in 1849, the Tawana were living at Toteng, at the south-western end of the lake. They were driven by the Kololo from the Kgwebe hills, their first home in Ngamiland after seceding from the Ngwato, and they actually endured a period of exile on the Chobe river as subjects of Sebetwane, chief of the Kololo. They escaped from this captivity in a destitute condition, having left all their cattle behind in their flight. But the Yei and the Kgalagadi living round Lake Ngami had plenty of cattle, and these they meekly surrendered to the Tawana, doubtless under threats of duress. It is probably at this time that the ascendancy of the Tawana and the subjection of the Yei, who had till then been treated as equals, began. During the next decade many traders and hunters travelled to Ngamiland, the wealth of the country, mainly in ivory, making the difficult journey across the Kgalagadi worth while.

In southern Bechuanaland, two of the four Rolong groups, the Tshidi and the Rratlou, were at Letlhakane and Khunwana respectively in the Molopo area south of Mafeking. When the Boers attacked Setshele at Dimawe in 1852, they demanded that the Tshidi Rolong should join in the campaign on their side. Montshiwa son of Tawana, chief of the Tshidi, refused the demand, whereupon the Boers launched an assault on Letlhakane. Montshiwa fled for sanctuary to the Ngwaketse and settled at Moshaneng. The Tshidi Rolong did not go back to the country south of the Molopo until 1877.

The southernmost Tswana tribe, the Tlhaping, with whom this story began, fell apart during the reign of Mothibi, and in the middle of the century was living in separate groups in the region of the Harts river under different members of the royal family. The group that will figure most prominently in this narrative was that settled at Taung.

Some tribes that later became autonomous had not yet acquired a country of their own. The Lete and the Tlokwa were living in the Kwena country as *protégés* of Setshele, while the Kgatla were still in the Transvaal.

Generally it can be said that the middle of the century was for the Tswana a period of recovery, of emergence from the confusion of the preceding years. In most tribes the administrative structure was once more cohesive, and the chiefs had regained their confidence and their authority. But the situation was still precarious and the future held many threats to this slowly returning stability.

IV · The Matabele and Kololo Missions — Troubled Times

In 1858 reinforcements arrived for the London Missionary Society in southern Africa. It was a party of four young missionaries, John Mackenzie, Roger Price, Thomas Morgan Thomas and William Sykes.

Prompted by Livingstone, the directors of the Society had decided to open two new stations in central Africa. One would be in the Zambezi valley where, says Livingstone, 'we have an immense region before us. Thousands live and die without God and without hope, though the command went forth of old, Go ye into all the world and preach the gospel to every creature'. As for the Kololo, he continues, 'they are by far the most savage race of people we have seen. But they treated us with uniform kindness, and would have been delighted had we been able to remain with them permanently'.[1] The new station would not only be a centre for the propagation of Christianity. It would also radiate a legitimate commerce as a counter to the slave trade, which was the curse of these lands. First, however, the Kololo must be persuaded to move from their unhealthy swamps to the uplands above the Zambezi; and this they would not do as long as they were threatened by the Matabele, against whom the swamps gave them protection. So it was decided that a mission must be established among the Matabele too. By means of the two allies, commerce and the Gospel, these two warlike peoples would be brought together to live side by side, and the wars that had plagued that part of Africa would come to an end.

The four new missionaries were therefore part of a two-pronged drive into central Africa. Morgan Thomas and Sykes would go to the Matabele, and Robert Moffat, because of his credit with Mzilikazi, would take them there. The Kololo party would be Mackenzie and Price, led by Holloway Helmore, an experienced missionary, but one whose career had been spent in healthy stations in southern Bechuanaland.

With the Matabele party was John Smith Moffat, a young man who was no stranger to Bechuanaland. He was the fourth son and eighth child of Robert, born at Kuruman in 1835 and schooled there by his mother until 1850 when, being destined to become a missionary, he was sent to England to be educated at seminaries belonging to the London Missionary Society. In June 1857 he was told to hold himself in readiness to go to Africa; but there was some delay in his eventual appointment, and his brother-in-law Livingstone, then on the eve of his Zambezi venture, from his own pocket enabled John to marry Emily Unwin and to set out as a free-lance missionary. Their son's defection from the beloved Society sorely grieved Robert and Mary Moffat, but John's participation in the Matabele expedition was no doubt an asset. He had Africa in the blood and he knew what to expect of African travel. Under Robert Moffat's expert guidance the party had a good journey and arrived safely in Matabeleland.

The expedition to the Kololo was not so fortunate. It was decided at the last moment that Mackenzie, whose wife was about to have a baby, should stay behind and go up with supplies the following year. Helmore and Price set off from Kuruman for the north in July 1859.

No proper precautions were taken for an enterprise of this kind. The expedition started much too late in the year, when the wells and pools on the route might be expected to be dry. Supplies were insufficient and the arrangements for storing drinking water inadequate. The equipment was incomplete and several essential articles were missing. The wagons were too few and they were much overloaded. The party included no medical man. The crowning folly was the decision that the men should be accompanied by their families – Mrs Helmore, with four children, and Mrs Price, who was pregnant. Indeed the latter gave birth to a baby girl at Letlhakane in the northern Kgalagadi while the travellers were still many miles from their destination.

After an appalling journey the missionaries struggled into Linyanti, capital of the Kololo, in February 1860. Here they expected to meet Livingstone, who they hoped would by that time have worked his way up the Zambezi from the east coast. But Livingstone was still far away downstream and did not arrive at Linyanti until the end of August.

Meanwhile the Kololo point blank refused to move their town to a healthier place and the party therefore decided to settle down temporarily where they were and begin the work of evangelization. But they all fell ill, probably of malaria, both Europeans and the Africans who had come with them, and presently they died one by one until of the Europeans only Price and two Helmore children were left. John Mackenzie, travelling towards the Chobe with supplies later in the year in accordance with the arrangements, found these survivors on the Boteti river and brought them back to Kuruman.[2]

The man who rescued the remains of the Kololo party was destined to play a crucial role in the history of Bechuanaland.[3] Like many of the agents of the London Missionary Society, John Mackenzie was a Scotsman from a humble home, child of a small farmer in Morayshire. He was sent at an early age to an unusual educational institution in Elgin, and from there was placed as apprentice with the proprietor of the local newspaper. At the age of eighteen he experienced a religious 'conversion' and resolved to become a missionary. After acceptance by the Society and a suitable course of training he sailed for South Africa in 1858. Before sailing he married Ellen Douglas, daughter of a church elder of Portobello near Edinburgh.

Following the Linyanti fiasco it was decided, after a period of some uncertainty, that Mackenzie's permanent station should be Shoshong, the capital of the Ngwato. Here he lived the normal life of the workaday missionary, preaching, teaching, healing, building and occupying himself in the hundred and one tasks that a man in his position was called upon to undertake. He was a witness of the Matabele raid on Shoshong in 1863, undertook one not very successful expedition to Matabeleland, developed a strong if realistic affection for the Tswana, and above all made a firm friend of Khama, the heir to the chiefship.

It was during Mackenzie's ministry at Shoshong that the divisive quarrels in the royal family erupted that were to split the tribe into warring factions. Of these troubles Mackenzie and his wife Ellen have each left an eye-witness account. Not unexpectedly they both support the Christian son against the heathen father.[4]

While at Shoshong Mackenzie made his first excursion into South African politics. In 1867 the German traveller Karl Mauch announced the discovery of gold in the Tati, an area claimed both by the Ngwato and the Matabele. On Mackenzie's recommendation Matsheng, at that time chief of the Ngwato, recognizing his own inability to control gold-diggers, wrote to the British High Commissioner, Sir Philip Wodehouse, asking that the gold-field might be taken under British protection. Shortly after, President M. W. Pretorius of the Transvaal, who had earlier importuned Matsheng for the cession of the Tati to the Transvaal, issued a proclamation annexing not only the new gold-field but also most of Bechuanaland, and in the east a corridor to the Indian Ocean. After protests from the British and the Portuguese the proclamation was withdrawn. On the other hand Matsheng's letter evoked little more than a courteous reply and the situation remained unchanged. However, interest in Tati gold soon shifted to newly-discovered Griqualand diamonds and the expected gold rush was a small one.

In 1868 the directors of the London Missionary Society invited the missionaries in South Africa to advise on new methods to 'call out the zeal and consecration of individuals'. The

Bechuanaland District Committee recommended that young Africans should be encouraged to become schoolmasters and teachers, and that a seminary under one of the local mission-aries should be established to train them. Returning in 1871 from a furlough in Britain during which he had published *Ten Years North of the Orange River*, Mackenzie found himself appointed, somewhat incongruously by ballot, to be tutor of the seminary. As a temporary measure work began at Shoshong, but in 1876 Mackenzie moved to Kuruman to work on buildings begun in 1875 by his colleague William Ashton. The seminary was called the Moffat Institution after the great Robert, and finance was provided by a fund raised in his honour when he retired in 1870.

In spite of labour troubles, difficulties in connection with land and the opposition of Mackenzie's colleague John Moffat, the walls of the Institution went up, and in two years there were solid buildings on the site. It is well that this was so. In 1878 a rising in southern Bechuanaland compelled the Europeans of the neighbourhood to take refuge in the Institution and Mackenzie found himself in command of a beleaguered citadel.

The troubles were deep-seated and went back many years. After 1852 differences among the Boers caused a relaxation of pressure on the Tswana tribes. When this pressure was resumed, the spark for open conflict was provided by the Tswana them-selves.

In 1857 a group of Tlhaping whose chief was Gasebone, profit-ing by the absence of the burghers who had gone to fight the Basuto, raided into Boer territory and came away with cattle and horses. The Boers quickly rallied, followed up the stolen cattle, killed Gasebone and his son Phohuetsile, took consider-able spoil and demanded of Mahura, chief of another group of Tlhaping, huge reparations in cattle, horses and guns. Mahura had already been well plundered by the commando and could not pay, whereupon the Boers convinced themselves that the

Kuruman missionaries were encouraging him to evade his obligations and there were rumours of a coming attack on the mission station. The missionaries at Kuruman, young and old, passed the first six months of 1859 in a state of apprehension. These anxieties caused the late departure of the Helmore–Price expedition to Linyanti and were hence in part responsible for the misfortunes that befell it.

Meanwhile tribal land was being steadily eaten away by encroachment from the Transvaal. 'About 1850', complained chief Montshiwa to the High Commissioner, 'one Boer after another took possession of the fountains and lands of the Barolong',[5] and other tribes were in no better case. Title was obtained in the most casual way. 'A settler seeking a new farm would ride out beyond the limits of known habitation, and seeing a portion of land that pleased him, would note the natural features that might be taken to define it. He would then go to the nearest Landdrost or Magistrate and claim the tract of land situated and bounded as he might describe it to be. Thereupon the Landdrost would give him a certificate of ownership.'[6] After this there would be an inspection, the farm would be advertised as about to be confirmed to the applicant, and if there were no protest within three months, the land became the property of the applicant.

That the land had been occupied and used by this tribe or that for generations mattered very little. There was always an effective way of getting rid of inconvenient tribesmen, which was to take exclusive possession of the wells. 'Land is next to useless', wrote Lieutenant-Colonel Moysey,

to blacks and whites alike, without water, and streams and water courses shewn in maps rarely exist, though the dry beds remain to show where not so many years ago there was water enough and to spare. The little that does remain near the fountain heads is usually monopolised by the Boer farmer, who has carefully selected his farm round the spring, and, by dams and water furrows, diverted the natural course of the water over his own land, where it runs to waste after having served his purpose.[7]

When the original inhabitants refused to budge, title would be issued just the same. 'It was the practice of the South African Republic to grant farms to its burghers and put them on the map while their occupation by Natives made it physically impossible for the grantees to take possession of them. Then the nominal owners would claim that Natives were squatting illegally on their farms.'[8]

The results of these haphazard yet callous proceedings were sometimes grotesque.

While on my way from Kuruman to Kimberley in October 1879 [wrote Mackenzie] I met a party of some forty or fifty white men armed and mounted – their waggons following on behind, containing ploughs, spades, etc. They had crossed the border when I saw them, but told me they had Government sanction, and were expecting the district magistrate to accompany them; and that they were on their way to select farms and to occupy them. . . . One of these enterprising men managed to elude Major Lowe's police, and was found by them, after complaint had been lodged by a native farmer, ploughing at one end of this native man's field, while the native was ploughing at the other.[9]

It was lucky for the native man that the area was at that time under British occupation.

Some farmers, perhaps more careful than others, took the trouble to obtain a formal grant from the local chief. These grants would be embodied in a document signed or rather marked by the chief and his councillors, or by some European calling himself the chief's authorized agent.

Such grants were doubly suspect. First, one has to ask oneself whether a complicated document in English, marked with crosses by an illiterate chief and his council and witnessed by friends of the beneficiary, is proof that the signatories had any idea what the transaction really was about. Secondly, had any African chief the power to alienate tribal land in perpetuity? The answer to each of these questions is surely no, and the whole concept of grants of this nature therefore stands condemned.

Unlike the British Government, which by the Sand River and Bloemfontein Conventions openly proclaimed their refusal to follow their migrant subjects all the way up Africa, the Government of the Transvaal was not in the least reluctant to absorb the lands that the burghers acquired. 'The worst feature of Transvaal policy is the reckless way in which, year after year, its Presidents have gone on proclaiming mere paper annexations of territories, which they have not and never can have the means of effectually governing. Nevertheless these annexations, based as they are upon hollow and fraudulent pretences, seriously affect the peace of South Africa.'[10] Such, for instance, was the all-embracing proclamation of President Pretorius in 1868. Such also was President Burgers' proclamation of 1874, when he annexed the whole of the territories of the Korana, the Rolong and the Tlhaping on the strength of alleged treaties made with puppet chiefs.[11]

The southern tribes, Rolong and Tlhaping, did not possess the internal unity that had enabled the northern Tswana to resist Boer strategy. 'In South Bechuanaland', records Mackenzie, 'I was met with different social conditions. I found that the power of the chiefs was very small indeed, and that the people had been divided and sub-divided by rival chiefs and headmen till the cohesion of the tribe, as such, was practically at an end.'[12]

In their perplexity the Tswana turned to the British for protection. In 1870, Lieutenant-General Hay, the Acting High Commissioner, writing about the ownership of the newly discovered diamond fields, said of the African parties to the dispute, who included the southern Tswana: 'Most [of the "original native inhabitants"] have long been desirous of placing themselves and their lands under the protection of Her Majesty's Government.'[13] This was confirmed by Sir Henry Barkly, the High Commissioner, a year later: 'It is true that one and all of the Chiefs concerned . . . are most anxious that their country should be taken under Her Majesty's protection.'[14] In 1879 Charles Warren, touring southern Bechuanaland after the disturbances which are described below, received requests from seven chiefs to be annexed by Britain.[15] Yet in 1882 Mankurwane, chief of the Tlhaping at Taung, was still desperately pleading for help. 'I thought that I was one flesh with the English, and we say that there is nothing so well knitted together as a piece of flesh; but now I am dying alone because I have always been for the English, and on that account have made myself many enemies.' And in a later letter: 'I again say, why am I forsaken, what fault have I done, that the English should forsake me?' Roper, Civil Commissioner at Kimberley, commented in forwarding Mankurwane's plea: 'It tells its own tale – to me, cognizant as I am of his fidelity to the British Government – a somewhat sad one.'[16]

However sad the tale, it left the British Government unmoved. It was not that the Colonial Office totally lacked sympathy towards the afflicted tribesmen. Well within twenty years of the Conventions, the Government had begun to regret them and in particular were considering a ban on the conveyance of arms and ammunition to the Boers beyond the borders of the Cape Colony.[17] One Colonial Secretary in 1866 read 'with great pain' of the 'nefarious practices' of the Boers (he was referring to the old charge of 'slave dealing' rather than to the more persistent process of land-grabbing).[18] Another agreed in 1876 that encroachment of Boers on Montshiwa's country was a question that was rapidly growing in importance and must shortly receive the most serious consideration of Her Majesty's Government.[19] Occasionally a permanent official would put up a resolute minute. 'These extra-Colonial South African questions', for instance wrote Robert Herbert, 'are full of awkwardness, but their difficulties are hardly ever diminished by submitting to the encroachments of the Republics.'[20] Generally, however, the policy is reflected in the Colonial Secretary's instructions to Sir Hercules Robinson when the latter took up his appointment as Governor of the Cape Colony and High Commissioner: 'I must . . . strongly impress upon you the necessity of not extending the responsibilities of this country beyond the present boundaries of Her Majesty's possessions.'[21] The annexation of areas adjacent to the Colonial frontier, when necessary, was the business of the Cape Colony, endowed with responsible government in 1872. It was no duty of the British taxpayer to 'redress the wrongs of African chiefs.

One opportunity did however present itself to bring some remedy to the land troubles on the Tswana border. Between 1869 and 1871 diamonds were found north and south of the Vaal river near its junction with the Harts, in land claimed by the Transvaal, the Orange Free State, and the indigenous tribes, Griqua, Tlhaping, and others. Barkly persuaded the Transvaal and the African claimants north of the Vaal to submit to arbitration. A commission sat at Bloemhof in 1871 and heard a mass of evidence. When the commissioners failed to agree the matter went to R. W. Keate, Lieutenant-Governor of Natal, for final arbitration. Keate's award was a compromise, as in the face of so many conflicting claims it was bound to be. But it did at least draw a line between the Transvaalers and the African tribes living to the west of them. That it proved ineffective, as we shall presently see, was not Keate's fault.[22]

Since President Brand of the Orange Free State had refused to go to arbitration, the Keate Award was not concerned with Free State claims. These were in respect of land on both sides of the Vaal, in country claimed by the Griqua chief, Nicholas Waterboer, one of the chiefs desirous of becoming British subjects. But in the course of his proceedings Keate had drawn a boundary from Platberg westwards between the Griqua and the Tlhaping which corresponded to the line claimed by the Griqua themselves. This seemed to Barkly to give colour to the whole Griqua case, and ten days after Keate's award, in accordance with Waterboer's wishes, he annexed the territory in dispute, diamonds and all.

In making his annexation the High Commissioner ignored a condition laid down by the British Government when giving him the necessary authority. It was that the Cape Colony should undertake responsibility for the cost and administration of the new acquisition. This in the event the Colonial Parliament refused to do, and the colony of Griqualand West remained an unwelcome commitment of the Imperial Government until it was incorporated in the Cape Colony in 1880.

Unhappily the annexation did nothing to help the former owners of the territory that was annexed. The Griqua, at whose instance and for whose benefit the annexation was ostensibly carried out, were probably past saving. During the preceding years they had been cajoled into parting with their land to Europeans in return for derisory payments and they had consequently become a landless proletariat. Waterboer himself was in the hands of land sharks and moneylenders, and his people's morale was undermined by drink. The new Government brought about no improvement. A land court set up under a young barrister named Andries Stockenstrom to unravel the mass of claims and counter-claims and claims that overlapped, was less than kind to the Griqua, although Stockenstrom must be given credit for destroying the pretensions of certain shady European agents and speculators. The Griqua continued to deteriorate morally and economically, so that by the end of the century they had lost the character of an organized community. Those that survived were working for Europeans.

The positive effects of the annexation were to check the southward expansion of the Boer republics, keep open the road to the north, and bring the diamond fields within the British Empire.[23]

The Keate Award threw up difficulties of its own. To the Boers, whose minds were set on the monopoly of the interior, the line drawn by Keate represented the loss of everything that the Great Trek was about, and they proceeded to evade it in all possible ways. The Transvaal Government made 'treaties' with chiefs described as 'paramount' but who were in reality only the heads of one or other of the sections of the Tlhaping and Rolong tribes. The Award itself was repudiated. Paper annexations were made on the basis of the bogus treaties. Individual farmers unrelentingly pursued 'that system of bullying and hard swearing on the part of the white occupants, by which the Boers have ever sought to drive natives from their land, and more particularly from their fountains'.[24]

Barkly did his best locally to counter Transvaal manoeuvres. At the same time he tried to persuade the Colonial Office to respond to the chiefs' requests for British protection. But the failure of the Cape legislature to incorporate Griqualand West was held against him, and the British Government was in no mood for further annexations. Alternatives were canvassed: the Transvaal to be told firmly that the British intended the Keate Award to be observed; encroachment to be prevented by force if necessary.[25] But, as Agar-Hamilton points out,[26] these were empty words. To refuse to annex was simply to encourage the farmers to come on. To restrain them with a force that would sooner or later be withdrawn, leaving the territory vacant again, was useless. There was no middle course between abandoning the threatened areas to the Boers and annexation.

Small wonder that the northern borders of the Cape were seething with discontent. John Mackenzie noted that 'the disturbances and wars which prevailed in Kaffirland in 1877 [the ninth Kaffir War] began to exert an influence even in a part of the country so distant as Griqualand West and Bechuanaland'.[27] Rumours found a fertile soil in which to propagate. Agents from the affected areas were urging the people to rise against the Europeans, telling them that the eastern tribes had won the war, that the white man was in flight, that tribal leaders were now occupying European farms and houses. Early in 1878 Mackenzie was warned of approaching trouble by a young chief. Disturbances broke out in May and a trader was murdered with his family in Griquatown. At the end of the month the massacre at Daniel's Kuil of the Burness family by household servants and Tlhaping caused all the Europeans of the region to concentrate at Kuruman, where they found accommodation in the unfinished buildings of the Moffat Institution.

The rising was of an unco-ordinated kind, and there was no common plan. By no means all the Tlhaping took part. Mankurwane held aloof, as did Jantje, Christian chief of the people living round Kuruman. But Jantje's son Luka was among the insurgents, as was Botlhasitse, chief of a section of the tribe living at Pokwane. Botlhasitse was the son of Gasebone, killed by the Boers in 1858, and he had himself been inveigled into signing a disastrous treaty in which he ceded his country and his people to the Transvaal. His participation in the disturbances is therefore not surprising.

A volunteer column raised to patrol the northern frontier of Griqualand West set out to relieve Kuruman and fell into a rebel ambush, suffering casualties. A larger force then made for Kuruman, raised the siege, and proceeded without difficulty to quell the rising.

As far as Bechuanaland is concerned the troubles of 1878–9 had two important consequences. The first was to bring together John Mackenzie and Charles Warren, a conjunction which, as we shall see, was of considerable significance in the history of the Bechuanaland Protectorate. The second was the existence for several years of a state of peace and good order in southern Bechuanaland, which was due to the presence near Kuruman of a small body of police left behind by the forces that came to quell the rising.

The annexation of the Transvaal by Great Britain in 1877 offered some respite to the harassed Tswana. The retrocession in 1881 at the end of the first Anglo-Boer war came to them as an unmitigated disaster. It was bad enough for the chiefs living west of the Transvaal who had helped the British during the war. Montshiwa sent his nephew Kebalepile to the High Commissioner: 'He will tell you', wrote the chief, 'that we are all very much grieved that the English Government are going to give the Transvaal back to the Boers, and that unless a strong line is made between the Boers and the natives, troubles will begin.'[28] It was even worse for the tribes living within the Transvaal: 'The chiefs are much dissatisfied and distressed at the country being returned and say that after experiencing British rule for four years they cannot live under the Boers again. They have returned to their homes as they say with heavy hearts and no hope for the future.'[29]

The Royal Commission which sat at Pretoria at the end of the war to meet the Boer leaders and 'to make diligent and full enquiry into all matters and things relating to the future settlement of the Transvaal territory' defined all the boundaries of the Transvaal for the first time. The western boundary was the work of Lieutenant-Colonel C. J. Moysey, who in 1879 had been appointed to investigate land claims in the Keate Award area, that is in the land *west* of the line drawn by Keate. The new boundary was admittedly a compromise but it conformed to the realities of the situation. It separated white from black, conceding to the Transvaal only that land that could be said to be in beneficial occupation by whites, even though it might have been occupied after the Keate Award and in contravention of it. Paper claims to so-called farms that had neither been occupied nor used were excluded.[30] If it can be argued that by accepting the new boundary the commission condoned blatant infractions of the Keate Award, it must also be conceded that the commissioners were working in the shadow of defeat and dared not risk more trouble with the Boers. It was not their fault that they had to play from weakness.

The Pretoria Convention, which was concluded on 3 August 1881, after carefully defining the new boundaries bound the Transvaal State, once more independent, strictly to adhere to them and to do its utmost 'to prevent any of its inhabitants from making any encroachments upon lands beyond the said State'. Thus by a stroke of the pen the Transvaal delegates renounced on behalf of their compatriots the habits of generations. It was really too much to expect that the undertaking would be taken seriously.

A more direct effect of the retrocession was the withdrawal of the little police force left behind in southern Bechuanaland after the troubles of 1878. This force had played a useful and unobtrusive part in maintaining order. 'Technically this was no more than "military occupation", but it supplied a Central Power around which all could gather, and which, however undefined and insufficient, was productive of much good.' The police left suddenly and without warning, whereupon, continues Mackenzie, 'Bechuanaland became what every confidential adviser and commissioner of Her Majesty had said it would become – the abode of anarchy, filibustering, and outrage.'[31]

V · John Mackenzie — The Protectorate

It was probably during his residence at Kuruman, in confrontation with the problems arising from European pressures on African tribes, that Mackenzie hammered out his ideas on African government. They were never officially accepted in his time and they brought upon him odium and even ridicule. But to later generations his ideas seem so obvious as to be almost axiomatic. The trouble was that he was twenty or thirty years in advance of those who made the final decisions on policy.

First, Mackenzie believed that the government of African peoples living next to a white colony was emphatically not the business of colonists, who of necessity must put their own interests first. It was a job for the Imperial Power, to be carried out through the agency of good British officers, educated, humane and with no axe to grind.

As a corollary to this, Mackenzie condemned the arrangement whereby the Governor of the Cape Colony was also High Commissioner and in that capacity the supreme authority in South Africa for the supervision of fringe areas inhabited mainly or wholly by black Africans. This duality in his function, thought Mackenzie, made the High Commissioner too responsive to the views and requirements of the Cape Colonists in his dealings with extra-Colonial territories. There should be a High Commissioner of the Crown in South Africa, who would be, as it were, 'a part of Downing Street in South Africa; and would be there to transact and to forward the business of the Imperial Government in that country'.[1] The colonial governors would continue to govern the colonies and administrators would run the black borderlands, but the High Commissioner, responsible only to London, would be the supreme authority.

His position would preserve him from 'close and daily contact
. . . with local politicians and their intrigues',[2] and he would
thus be able impartially to do justice to both white and black.
It is arguable that at least one specific misfortune in the life of
the Protectorate might have been avoided (or at least less
damage done) if Mackenzie's advice had been heeded (see
pp. 149–50).

Mackenzie regarded the northward march of the European as
inevitable and in some respects desirable. As a man of his time
he had great faith in the civilizing mission of the white races.
But, he said, the European advance must be regulated and
contained. There must be no disorderly land-grabbing. Aliena-
ation of land to Europeans must only take place after sufficient
space had been assured to the African. Moreover the Europeans
must be good Europeans, 'combining to make a new and wild
country the home of Christian peace and refinement, as well as
prosperity'.[3] He thought that land tenure for Africans should
be individual, as giving the occupier an incentive to good husbandry, but that the title should not be transferable.

It goes without saying that Mackenzie was totally against
discrimination between people on grounds of colour, pointing
out that in South Africa there were native peoples lighter in
colour than many southern Europeans. 'Of what colour', he
asks, 'was that beloved and adored Jewish Teacher who was
crucified at Jerusalem by a provincial Roman Governor, dying
a death inflicted only on people belonging to "inferior races",
and never on one of the superior or "conquering race", when he
was sentenced to death?'[4]

Mackenzie was always at pains to demonstrate that the
Tswana were by no means ignorant and primitive. On the
contrary, they had reached a respectable degree of civilization
and would be perfectly well able to support a modest administration. At the same time government must be of a simple kind
and the laws such as the people could understand.

As regards the troubles besetting the Tswana at that time,

Mackenzie believed that the Imperial Government should respond without ado to the chiefs' request for British protection. Sooner or later, he said, Great Britain would have to step in: 'Responsibility is thrust upon the English Government in Southern Africa. It is impossible to avoid it except by abandoning the country altogether.'[5] The longer intervention was delayed the more expensive it would be. Why wait for the situation to deteriorate still further? 'It would be difficult to prove that it is our interest to wait until a great many more thefts have taken place in Bechuanaland, more blood has been shed, and some crowning outrage has been committed, and then undertake the government of the country in question. The chiefs offer that government now, and profess their inability. Why not accept what will certainly be ours in the long run before the usual outrages have taken place?'[6]

The supreme Power in South Africa, said Mackenzie, must be Britain, and he dreamt of a protectorate that would reach to the Zambezi, part of a great dominion of Austral Africa under the British Crown. He envisaged something in the nature of a confederation of white colonies and black protectorates, the whites self-governing, the blacks under a more informal administration which he called territorial. The unifying factor, attracting the common loyalty of all, would be the Imperial Government. It was a noble and in some respects prophetic vision. If Mackenzie could write, 'the future of South Africa is not in the hands of the Transvaal', at the same time assuming too easily that the Boer republic would be prepared to form part of a British-dominated federation, it must be remembered that he was thinking and writing before mineral discoveries and subsequent industrial development had made the Transvaal the focus of economic power in South Africa.

All these arguments Mackenzie pressed on the two officers in charge of the operations in 1878, Owen Lanyon, Administrator of Griqualand West, and Charles Warren. They became zealous converts and warmly advocated British intervention in their

despatches to higher authority. Mackenzie was all this time acting as unofficial political adviser to the forces of occupation,
and in 1879 Barkly's successor Sir Bartle Frere offered him the
post of commissioner for the occupied zone. But Mackenzie
would not abandon his vocation of missionary and the London
Missionary Society would not allow him to combine the duties
of missionary and administrator, so the proposal fell through.
At the same time Frere's own recommendation that a British
protectorate be established west of the Transvaal was firmly
turned down by the Colonial Office. In 1882 Mackenzie went on
furlough to campaign for his ideas in England.

The trouble on the border was aggravated, indeed partly
caused, by dissensions among the Tswana themselves. Montshiwa, chief of the Tshidi Rolong, was at odds with his neighbours Moswete and Matlhaba, chiefs respectively of the Rratlou
and Rrapulana sections of the tribe. Montshiwa had been loyal
to the British during the recent Anglo-Boer war whereas
Moswete, who was in fact a creature of the Boers, took the
Transvaal side. Fighting between Montshiwa and his enemies
broke out in 1881 and continued sporadically, an affair of raids
and counter-raids, at first without conclusive results. Further
south Mankurwane was quarrelling with Mosweu, chief of the
Korana, who was supported by the Transvaalers. When
Mosweu joined Moswete and Matlhaba against Montshiwa,
Mankurwane attempted to relieve pressure on the latter by
attacking the Korana town of Mamusa. This plunged him into
hostilities with Mosweu.

No great harm might have come of all this if Moswete and
Mosweu had not taken the fatal step of enlisting white 'volunteers' to fight their battles for them. These were mercenaries
who had been persuaded to give their services by promises of
eventual land grants in Montshiwa's and Mankurwane's countries. The leader of Moswete's volunteers was Nicholas Gey van
Pittius, a prominent citizen of the Transvaal. Mosweu's volunteers were led by G. J. van Niekerk. Neither Mankurwane nor

Montshiwa had a white army of this kind, and when an attempt
was made to engage volunteers to fight for Mankurwane the
Cape Government promptly stopped recruitment by using the
Foreign Enlistment Act. Similarly, when at the beginning of
1882 Mankurwane's European agent asked for permission to
buy ammunition in the Colony the request was refused, because, came the reply, 'the Government desire to preserve
strict neutrality'.[7] A request for the same facilities by Montshiwa also met with no success.

The situation of Montshiwa and Mankurwane soon became
desperate. Their territories were raided daily, the well-armed
aggressors retreating into the Transvaal with their booty.
Early in February 1882 the High Commissioner, Sir Hercules
Robinson, reported to London that Moswete had overpowered
Montshiwa and laid waste his territory.

> He [Moswete] has at present about 80 Boers fighting for him
> as volunteers; this number will shortly be considerably in-
> creased, as recruiting [is] actively going on in [the] Transvaal.
> The volunteers have three ship's guns with them; two of
> their headmen are members of [the] Volksraad, and, with
> others, have drawn up on behalf of [the] volunteers, an
> agreement with Moshette [Moswete] that, for their services,
> they are to receive half the booty and all Montsioa's [Mont-
> shiwa's] ground south of [the] Maloppo [Molopo] river,
> should they succeed in expelling him.[8]

Mankurwane was in no better case. In April 1882 the missionary William Ashton foretold a famine among the Tlhaping
as a result of Boer depredations, and in May the trader H. W.
Jarvis reported to Major Stanley Lowe, then commanding the
Border Police at Boetsap in Griqualand West, that the Boers
were sweeping off all Mankurwane's cattle and the cattle of the
neighbouring Tlharo tribe.[9] In August Mankurwane was *in
extremis* and made the best peace he could with his enemies,
accepting the 'protection' of the Transvaal and yielding a large

area in his country to be carved into farms for Mosweu's volunteers.[10]

To the chiefs' appeals for help the British Government's reply was negative. The High Commissioner accurately reflects Colonial Office attitudes when, writing in June 1882, he says, 'It is very painful to be obliged to disregard such appeals for help [from chiefs] who have always been amenable to our influence and proved themselves our faithful allies in time of trouble; but it appears to me that unless their territory were annexed, or a British protectorate established over it, neither the Imperial Government nor the Colony can do more than has now been done to ensure the independent chiefs in Bechuanaland being left unmolested.' The Colony, he went on to say, was wholly unwilling to intervene, and he believed that the British Government 'would not be disposed to establish a Protectorate over the territory in question, as such a step would involve the perpetual risk of having to protect the native tribes in it from European adventurers by the employment of an Imperial force'.[11]

Robinson's belief was correct. 'The Cape Government and Legislature will not interfere', wrote Herbert in the Colonial Office, 'and we cannot establish an Imperial Protectorate in this district; so the Boers will probably get possession of the country.'[12] The Colonial Secretary was no more hopeful. 'There is no real remedy for this', wrote Lord Kimberley, 'but the annexation of the country, a remedy which in my opinion would be worse than the disease.'[13] Having had one war with the Boers, the British Government were not disposed to risk another.

There was nothing to be hoped for from Britain and in October 1882 Montshiwa, his people exhausted by famine and disease, followed Mankurwane's example and signed a treaty dictated by the marauders, in which he recognized his subjection to the Transvaal and gave up all his country south of the Molopo river, ostensibly to the freebooters' stalking horse Moswete, but in reality as a battle trophy for Moswete's volunteers.[14] Thus in hardly more than a year after the Pretoria Convention, substantial infractions of the boundary clauses had taken place, certainly with the complicity of the Transvaal Government and without effective reaction from Britain.

Towards the end of 1882 the map of southern Africa was embellished by the addition of two new republics. Goshen was founded by Moswete's volunteers under van Pittius and was a nest of robbers at Rooigrond west of Mafeking. Stellaland was established by Mosweu's volunteers under van Niekerk round a town which they called Vryburg in the heart of the country of the Tlhaping. It was based on titles to land granted by Mosweu in Mankurwane's territory. Both republics had the support of the Transvaal, and both lay on the coveted north road to the interior.

Meanwhile in England Mackenzie was fighting against heavy odds. The Government, beset with trouble in Egypt and as usual in Ireland, was steadily opposed to the expense and complications of direct intervention in southern Africa. The public was disenchanted with 'colonial adventures' after the disasters in Afghanistan and at Isandhlwana. The press was hostile or indifferent, and at best ill-informed. However there was a sympathetic minority in Parliament led by W. E. Forster, and Mackenzie found support among humanitarians and philanthropists throughout the country. A group of prominent people interested in Africa came together to constitute an informal body which called itself the South African Committee. The object of the committee was to hold public meetings, lobby important people, influence the press and generally to mobilize public opinion.

The first shots in Mackenzie's campaign were fired at a meeting called by the London Missionary Society at the Westminster Palace Hotel on 25 July 1882. Mackenzie addressed the meeting and hammered away at his usual themes: the civilized condition of the Tswana, their relations with Great Britain, their desire for British protection, Boer encroachment and the rape of

Tswana land, the inertia of British authority. The speech was printed and circulated as a pamphlet.

Thereafter Mackenzie stumped the length and breadth of England addressing meetings organized by the Society. Not content with oratory he lobbied the press, seeking out influential editors to enlist their support, and writing articles of his own to newspapers and periodicals. He also stormed the citadel, using as his weapon a pamphlet entitled 'Bechwanaland [sic],* the Transvaal and England: a statement and a plea', which he sent to Lord Kimberley and to Mr Gladstone.

The *Pall Mall Gazette*, whose editor, W. T. Stead, became a zealous ally, carried an oft-quoted description of Mackenzie's activity at that period: 'At missionary meetings, lecture rooms, and in public meetings, he set to work to make them [his fellow-countrymen] see the facts. . . . He had never done writing . . . there seemed no limit to his activity. He interviewed Cabinet Ministers, he buttonholed editors, he haunted the lobby of the House of Commons. He saw everyone who had any influence in the matter, and compassed sea and land if by any means he might make one proselyte.'[15]

But it was disappointing work. The Government of Mr Gladstone, dedicated to peace and economy, could hardly be expected to give way to a fanatical missionary who seemed determined to involve the country in a new Boer war. So the year 1883 passed inconclusively, the Colonial Office still unwilling to take action, while Parliament, in the course of unsatisfactory debates, gave no indication as to what the Government was likely to do.

In the midst of all his other preoccupations Mackenzie found time to write another book, *Day Dawn in Dark Places*, an account of missionary life intended for young people.

The Transvaal Volksraad (Assembly) had ratified the Pretoria Convention with much reluctance and had always resented the

* Mackenzie often uses this spelling.

boundary line. The Boers yearned for a return to the easy conditions of the Sand River Convention, 'which then made an end
of troubles, and became the foundation of our freedom and
independence'.[16] About the middle of 1883 the Transvaal
Government sent a deputation to London headed by the shrewd,
rough-hewn President, Paul Kruger, to discuss the Pretoria
Convention and to seek modifications. The deputation's main
complaint was the western boundary. This, they said, cut tribes
in half and was the cause of anarchy on the border. It soon
became clear that what the deputation wanted was complete
control of the road to the north and of the whole of the country
of Montshiwa and Mankurwane.

It was fortunate that Sir Hercules Robinson was in London
for consultations and he made short work of the deputation's
claims. To remove the curbs on the trekking habits of the Boers,
he said, would simply mean that tribe after tribe would successively be absorbed in the Transvaal, whose ultimate boundaries
would be the Indian and Atlantic Oceans. Independent tribes
would be extinguished, and communications between the Cape
Colony and the interior of Africa would be effectively barred.
No faith whatever should be placed in Transvaal guarantees for
the security of African interests. 'Experience has led me', he
wrote, 'to doubt the practical efficacy of such "guarantees" so
long as there are native cattle to be stolen or native lands that
are worth appropriating.'[17]

Robinson went on boldly to propose that a British Commissioner should be posted to southern Bechuanaland to maintain
order on the frontier and to act as friend and adviser to the
chiefs.

Robinson's emphatic advice weighed heavily in the scale.
Although Kruger and his colleagues put up a dour fight, Lord
Derby, the Colonial Secretary, stood his ground. Moswete and
Mosweu were abandoned to the Transvaal, whose puppets they
were, but the new boundary was drawn east of the road to the
north. This had the double advantage of saving the road itself

from the risk of being closed, at the same time preserving the remaining land of Montshiwa and Mankurwane.

After much tough bargaining in which Robinson played a leading part the London Convention was signed on 27 February 1884. The most important clauses were certainly the ones defining the new boundary. Others included concessions to Transvaal *amour-propre*: the Convention dropped all reference to the suzerainty of the Queen, a controversial expression which appeared in the Pretoria Convention and was much resented by the Boers; the British Resident in the Transvaal whom the Pretoria Convention had established there as a sort of watch-dog for the African population would be replaced by a lesser official; the term 'Transvaal State' was abolished and the old 'South African Republic' restored. More immediately practical was the reduction of the Transvaal debt to Britain and of the interest on it.

Complementary to the Convention was the decision to establish a protectorate in the country 'outside' the Transvaal. This loose term meant in effect southern Bechuanaland, which then consisted mainly of Stellaland and Goshen and the truncated areas still remaining to the Tlhaping and Rolong living west of the new boundary of the South African Republic. The British Government's decision was largely determined by a sort of promise from Thomas Scanlen, Prime Minister of the Cape Colony, which in the end was to prove illusory, that the Colony would share the cost. The question now arose of appointing an officer to administer the Protectorate, and again Robinson came to the rescue. Somewhat to the surprise of the Colonial Office the High Commissioner recommended Mackenzie, who, he said, was 'by far the best fitted for the post'. With Mackenzie's ambitious schemes for local administration in mind the Colonial Office had misgivings but nevertheless approved.

Mackenzie had been very active during the negotiations that had led to the London Convention. He had greeted the arrival of the Transvaal deputation with a broadside in the *Pall Mall*

Gazette, in which he stated clearly that the object of the Transvaal was nothing less than the political supremacy of South Africa, to which Bechuanaland was the key. Thereafter he continued his propaganda without respite, in the press, on the public platform and in the Colonial Office, where he was an assiduous visitor. The Convention, when it came, fell short of what he thought was just and wise but the establishment of a protectorate represented in some measure the vindication of all that he and his allies, Frere, Lanyon, Warren and others, had said and written, hitherto in vain. He sailed for South Africa in March 1884 and on arrival in Cape Town duly received his commission as Deputy Commissioner in Bechuanaland.[18]

If Mackenzie's appointment had been made in 1879, at the time when Frere was pressing for British Commissioners on the border, it might have been wholly successful, and the country would thereby have been spared much tribulation. As it was the decision came too late. By 1884 freebooters and land sharks had poured into the vacuum created by the withdrawal of the police in 1881, the tribes were impoverished and demoralized, while the Transvaal, having evaded one convention successfully for three years, knew all the dodges necessary to evade a new one. Mackenzie might still have pulled it off if he had been given the force to do it. But the Colonial Office and the High Commissioner seem to have envisaged nothing more than a short holding operation until the country could be handed to the Cape, and even then they both seriously underplayed the difficulties. In this they were encouraged by grotesquely euphoric reports from Robinson's Imperial Secretary, Graham Bower, who visited Bechuanaland just before Mackenzie's arrival.[19] In reality the task that faced the Deputy Commissioner was to set up a proper administration in Stellaland, enquire into several hundred doubtful land titles, eject squatters, rehabilitate the ruined tribesmen and prepare them for taxation, prevent tribal wars, and finally drive out the men of

Goshen, a gang of brigands who had the determined backing of the Transvaal. To accomplish this he had at the outset one experienced assistant, Major Lowe, and ten locally-recruited policemen. If this number were insufficient he might raise it to twenty-five.

Even if Mackenzie had been able to overcome the problem of his lack of force, there were influences working against him which in the end proved irresistible. These operated at the very seat of power in Cape Town.

Mackenzie's appointment had been received in South Africa with widespread disapproval. His vocation as an agent of the London Missionary Society made him suspect to people among whom the memory of John Philip was still sour, while his own position on questions affecting African rights was hardly calculated to enhance his popularity. Moreover the Cape Government, because of links between the Cape Dutch and the Transvaal Boers, would do nothing to offend the Transvaal.

Above all, there was Cecil Rhodes, a coming man, making his fortune in Kimberley and his mark in Cape politics. Rhodes and Mackenzie had this in common, that they both dreamt of British expansion (though Rhodes's ideas, unlike Mackenzie's, did not stop at the Zambezi) and both believed that the key to supremacy in South Africa lay in control of the lands lying west of the Transvaal. But to Rhodes the agency of expansion was not the 'Imperial factor', which he despised profoundly, but the Cape Colony. 'One lesson had been burned into his understanding, that neither the Colonial Office nor the British Cabinet could be trusted to carry through any policy of expansion, nor even to maintain the dignity and honour of the British name. Whatever he wished to achieve must be done by his own effort, and with other instruments.'[20]

This suited the Colonial Office, where opinion was still set against extending imperial responsibilities. 'Once we get Natives under the management of the much abused Cape Colonists,' wrote Edward Fairfield, 'and leave the Cape Colonists alone, everything goes right. They understand Native management much better than we do.' Fairfield's superior Herbert, though critical of British policy in South Africa as it was conducted by High Commissioners connected with Colonial governments ('very unsuccessful and costly'), nevertheless did not rebut the Colonial principle.[21] Subsequent events were to show that the Tswana had little more to expect from the Colony than from the Transvaal.

Rhodes and Mackenzie, though they both wanted the same thing, were bound to be in opposition as to the means of obtaining it. This for Mackenzie was bad enough. It was made worse by the attitude of the High Commissioner, who, apparently a staunch Imperial Ruler in England, was now a wholehearted supporter of the Colonial school:

> The idea of the permanent presence of the Imperial factor in the interior – of a South African India in the Kalahari – is simply an absurdity. . . . All the Imperial Government can now do in South Africa is, by means of spheres of influence, protectorates, and Crown Colonies, to gradually prepare the way for handing native territories over to the Cape and Natal so soon as such transfers can be made with justice to the natives, and advantage to all concerned.[22]

The Robinson–Rhodes policy, at whatever cost to the local tribes, was now a quick settlement with the Stellalanders, who were by this time considered to be immovable. To effect this, the High Commissioner was prepared to give van Niekerk's followers almost anything if they would only keep quiet and allow themselves to be annexed to the Colony.

Robinson had other problems. There had been a change of government at the Cape and the new Ministry shied away from Scanlen's promise to bear part of the cost of the Protectorate. In fact the Ministers showed little sign that they shared Rhodes's enthusiasm for the north, and it was clear that the Colony, no less than the Stellalanders, needed to be coaxed into the

British Government's view that the Protectorate was an exclusively Colonial interest, and that it was up to the Cape
Colony to shoulder the responsibility for it.

The story of Mackenzie's brief mission is a painful one which
has been told several times.[23] He failed because he was not given
the time or the power to enable him to succeed. Most of his
actions were on the face of them wise and honourable and those
(comparatively unimportant) measures that have been most
criticized will be found on analysis to have been dictated by the
paucity of means at his disposal.

Mackenzie arrived in the Protectorate at the end of April
1884. He obtained cessions of jurisdiction from the Tlhaping
and Rolong chiefs; proclaimed the Queen's authority; made
more or less satisfactory arrangements for governing Stellaland,
appointing none other than former 'Administrator' van
Niekerk as his Assistant Commissioner (the idea originated in
the Colonial Office); and began under difficulties to build up a
police force. At Rooigrond he was rebuffed by the Goshenites,
who continued their depredations in Montshiwa's country
under the Deputy Commissioner's nose. At Montshiwa's request
he appointed an Assistant Commissioner, J. M. Wright, to stay
with the chief in Mafeking.

On the burning question of land titles in Stellaland, Mackenzie went as far as he reasonably could to reassure the holders.
All land matters, he said, would come before a court. As a
matter of personal opinion he thought that all volunteers would
get their farms or compensation in money or land. At the same
time he routed some of the land sharks and speculators who
surrounded chief Mankurwane.

During Mackenzie's absence in Montshiwa's country the
arrangements that he had made in Stellaland collapsed. Van
Niekerk ran out on him, taking with him about half the white
community, the so-called 'Patriots'. But the 'Loyals', that is
the half that remained in Vryburg, continued to give their
Deputy Commissioner quite solid backing.

In spite of van Niekerk's secession Mackenzie was not dissatisfied with the way things were shaping, but his enemies were busy in Cape Town. The rift in Stellaland between Patriots and Loyals was seized upon as evidence of the threat of another 'race war'. It was said that the majority of Stellalanders disliked Mackenzie's rule; that his 'land settlement' had given great dissatisfaction to all concerned; that more trouble was to be expected. The Cape Ministers told Robinson that Mackenzie's continuance in office was 'the most serious, if not the only obstacle to the maintenance of peace in the Protectorate', and the Transvaal Government wrote to urge his withdrawal as 'the first step towards coming to a proper regulation of matters'. Finally Robinson, worn down by the lobbying of Rhodes and Bower and by the importunities of the Cape politicians, called the Deputy Commissioner to Cape Town for discussions and showed him the hostile correspondence from the Ministers and from the Transvaal. On 19 August Mackenzie resigned and Rhodes was appointed in his stead.

While Mackenzie was on his way to Cape Town for the discussions which were to end in his resignation, a message from Wright, his assistant in Mafeking, brought the worst news that had yet come from Goshen. On 28 July the freebooters made a grand sweep into the Ngwaketse country, lifting 3000 head of cattle. Three days later they came back past Mafeking and the Rolong rushed out to recover the cattle of their allies. In the battle that followed a hundred of Montshiwa's men died, including Christopher Bethell, a fiery, quixotic young Englishman who had been stationed in the area during the events of 1878–9 and had stayed on afterwards, giving himself wholeheartedly to the defence of the tribe.

Rhodes was rebuffed by the Goshenites as decisively and much more contemptuously than had been his predecessor, but he arranged matters amicably in Stellaland by cancelling all Mackenzie's transactions and by confirming without question the volunteers' land titles. In Stellaland, as in Goshen, the freebooters had triumphed and Mackenzie's hopes lay in ruins.

As if to celebrate their victory over Rhodes the Goshenites forced Montshiwa into another disastrous treaty in which he gave himself and his people unconditionally to Goshen and surrendered most of his remaining land. The crowning rejection of the London Convention was a provisional proclamation by Kruger that chiefs Montshiwa and Moswete were under the 'protection and control' of the South African Republic. (By 'provisional' Kruger said that he meant that he would withdraw it if the British Government objected to it.) With the proclamation was published a letter from Montshiwa, renouncing Mackenzie and all his works.

In killing Bethell the Goshenites committed more than a crime. It was also a blunder. People in England were indignant at the death in circumstances almost amounting to murder of a brave young Englishman 'in an obscure struggle'. It was while public opinion was still sensitive on the subject that Kruger chose to issue his annexation proclamation and the Reverend S. J. du Toit ran up the flag of the South African Republic at Rooigrond. This was too much even for the long-suffering British Government and it was decided to send a military expedition to Bechuanaland. Charles Warren, Mackenzie's old friend of 1878–9, was chosen to command it.

VI · The Warren Expedition

While the events related in the last chapter were taking place in southern Bechuanaland, the northern Tswana remained comparatively unmolested, although from time to time distracted by troublesome domestic questions.

The three great tribes, Kwena, Ngwato and Ngwaketse, were living broadly in the areas in which they had originally settled. Setshele, still restless and active, ruled the Kwena, helped by his son Sebele. Khama was now firmly in the saddle as chief of the Ngwato. Gaseitsiwe, a less forceful character than either Setshele or Khama, was chief of the Ngwaketse. He was helped by his son Bathoen, who was destined to become chief of the tribe on the death of Gaseitsiwe in 1889.

The territories of the Kwena and the Ngwaketse had to some extent become eroded by the occupation of land on the eastern side by recent immigrants. In 1869 the Kgatla under chief Kgamanyane, hitherto living in the Transvaal, fled from the Boers and in 1871 settled at Mochudi in Kwena territory. This led to trouble with Setshele, who demanded that the Kgatla should pay him tribute in recognition of their occupation of part of his country. There was some reason for this demand since Mochudi had once been the home of the Kwena and was named after Kgabo's successor Motshodi. However the Kgatla refused to pay tribute, claiming to be independent, and in 1875 Setshele sent an army against them under his son Sebele, which was bloodily repulsed. Periodic outbreaks of fighting continued for some years and the dispute was not finally settled until 1899 with the fixing of the tribal boundaries. Similarly the Lete, since 1852 dependents of the Kwena, had difficulty in establishing their independence when they moved to Ramotswa in 1875, in country which the Ngwaketse claimed as theirs. Gaseitsiwe sent an army under Bathoen to oust them, but an attack on Ramotswa was repulsed with heavy losses.

The Tlokwa returned from the Transvaal about 1884 under their chief Gaborone, who received from Letshele a small space on the eastern edge of the Kwena country for his tribe to live in.

The Ngwaketse had not altogether escaped the attentions of the freebooters. That the chiefs were conscious of the need for a united front is shown by a sort of defensive alliance between Setshele, Montshiwa and Gaseitsiwe in 1883.[1] But this did not prevent the disastrous raid of 1884 which started with the robbery of Ngwaketse cattle and ended in the death of Montshiwa's valuable adjutant Bethell. Had the British Government not stood firm on the London Convention, Gaseitsiwe would probably have gone the way of Montshiwa and Mankurwane.

Away in the north-west the Tawana of Ngamiland had enemies other than Boers to contend with. In 1882 and again in 1884 they were raided by Matabele. The first campaign was inconclusive, although the Matabele lifted a great deal of stock, but in 1884 the Tawana assembled all their cattle on an island in the Okavango swamps and waited in the swamps for the invading army. The Matabele found themselves on unfamiliar terrain and suffered very large casualties, many from drowning. They did not worry the Tawana again.

The definitive emergence of Khama as chief of the Ngwato was the most significant development among the northern Tswana. With his father Sekgoma in exile in the Kwena country, he had become chief in 1872, but not for long. His brother Kgamane intrigued against him, and in 1873 Khama called back Sekgoma to take up the chiefship once more. After a few uneasy months he himself moved with his followers from Shoshong to the Boteti river where he stayed until 1875. In that year he returned to Shoshong with all his people and belongings and took over the chiefship for good and all. Sekgoma and Kgamane fled once again to the Kwena country and were only allowed to return after Khama was firmly in the saddle. Sek-goma's tumultuous life came to an end in Serowe in 1883.

As soon as he had made himself safe in his position, Khama proceeded energetically to reform the tribe. One of his first acts was to prohibit alcoholic drink. Then all the traditional rites and ceremonies offensive to his Christian conscience, such as initiation, rainmaking and so on, were discountenanced or abolished. More harmful practices like witchcraft, excessive game destruction and the maltreatment of subordinate peoples were also discouraged. He co-operated heartily with the missionaries, built schools and fostered education. His honesty was complete, his purpose lofty and his devotion to the interests of his people as he saw them was absolute.

The medal had its reverse side. Khama was intolerant, autocratic, and ruthless, so it was said, towards any form of opposition. He was suspicious of any of his tribesmen whom he thought was becoming rich or powerful, and he could be vindictive, as witness his feuds with his son Sekgoma and other relatives. On the other hand one must ask oneself whether a more flexible, less determined character would have succeeded, as Khama did, in playing at that time a decisive, and for the most part beneficent role in the affairs of this part of Africa.

By 1885 the London Missionary Society was well established in the country north of the Molopo, and there were stations at Kanye, Molepolole, Shoshong, and at Inyati in Matabeleland. J. D. Hepburn had made strenuous efforts to establish a station among the Tawana, but the first Ngamiland Church received its death blow in 1886, when chief Moremi publicly renounced Christianity and ordered the missionary out of the country.

As the Society extended northwards the missionaries' position became one of considerable influence. The Tswana were up against new forces with which they were unfamiliar and with which they were unable to deal by themselves. There were Boers and Matabele, who must be resisted and if possible repelled. Then there were traders, hunters, prospectors, miners, concession-hunters, all of whom wanted something from the harassed chiefs. To cap it all there were European governments, of great but apparently capricious strength, whose intentions were more difficult to read than any. The missionaries understood what these people wanted, and they were the only ones who wanted nothing for themselves. Moreover the missionaries had power. They could talk to Europeans and even to governments on equal terms, and the Tswana noticed very soon that the missionaries would always employ their power on behalf of the people to whom they ministered. It was inevitable that the chiefs should turn to them for guidance in all their dealings with strangers. With the declaration of the Protectorate and with the appointment in due course of European civil servants, the missionaries' political functions were gradually absorbed by administrators. Nevertheless they continued almost to the end of the century to double the role of spiritual mentor and political adviser; and in secular matters they remained the necessary intermediaries between the chiefs and the British authorities.

As the century wore on the importance of Kuruman declined. The establishment of stations extending up to Matabeleland left Moffat's old station almost on the southern edge of the area which it sought to serve. Not only was Kuruman too far south, it was also too far west. In early days when it marked the northern limit of European settlement the mission was an indispensable stage on the road to the interior, where travellers could find rest and refreshment, replenish their supplies, remedy deficiencies in transport and generally prepare for the difficult journey ahead. As time went on, new roads were opened further east, and the railway that reached Mafeking in 1895 ran through Vryburg, almost eighty miles from Kuruman. The mission now became one among a number, without the advantage possessed by the others of being at a large tribal centre.

The same factors affected the Moffat Institution, on which had been spent so much money and labour. Remote from communications and from any good scholastic 'catchment area', the

Institution struggled on for some years, finally closing down in 1897 to be replaced by a new institution at Tiger Kloof, a few miles south of Vryburg.

The London Missionary Society was not the only mission in the field. The Dutch Reformed Church had worked among the Kgatla since 1864 and established a mission at Mochudi in the 'seventies after the tribe had settled there as newcomers from the Transvaal. The Roman Catholics, Church of England, United Free Church of Scotland and Seventh Day Adventists are more recent arrivals in Bechuanaland.

Commercially the early 'eighties were a period of stagnation and the character of trade was undergoing change. When the first explorers visited the Tswana the domestic economy was a simple one based on local products and manufactures. This was soon influenced by new factors, especially by the introduction of European trade goods. The first words of chief Mothibi to the missionaries Evans and Hamilton were, 'What have you brought for barter?', and neither the chief nor his councillors were at all pleased to learn that the visitors had not come to trade.[2]

The articles most eagerly sought by Africans were guns and ammunition. Most of the guns sold to tribesmen were flimsy and badly made but the trade was an extensive one in spite of efforts by the neighbouring Boers to stop it. (The ultimate in the African arms trade was the sale to Lobengula by the traders Finaughty and Deans of two old ship's cannons.[3]) Other trade goods included cloth and clothing, salt, blankets, brassware, hoes, snuff boxes, cooking utensils, knives, beads and tobacco.

In return for these articles traders obtained ivory, cattle, and hunting trophies such as skins and ostrich feathers. The profits to the trader were at first very high. In 1849 J. H. Wilson bought ten large elephant tusks in Ngamiland, where ivory was regarded as useless bone, for a trade gun worth thirteen shillings. As late as the early 1860s prices still remained very low. A tusk might be obtained for a snuff box and a sheep for a few beads.[4]

But the tribesmen duly learnt the value of their wares and

began to ask more for them. At the same time the trade in
ivory declined as the persecuted elephants retreated into in-
accessible tsetse country, and the exploitation of new com-
modities was not yet fully developed. At Shoshong traders'
stores, nine in 1879 with twenty-three traders and their families,
had fallen to six in six years, and even these were not doing well.
'I have it on the authority of one of the oldest traders in the
town', noted Lieutenant E. A. Maund in 1885, 'that there is not
an export trade of more than £15,000 yearly at the present time,
whereas in the palmy days, one firm alone (Francis and Clark)
had a trade of £50,000.' [5] The northward drive of the British
South Africa Company in due course brought a revival of
commercial activity along the route, and meanwhile the
Tswana had already begun to replace barter in tusks and
feathers with a money economy.

Tati, scene of the gold discovery that had caused Matsheng
to ask for British help, had fallen on bad times after the first
brief period of prosperity. The gold was reef gold, requiring the
use of heavy machinery and equipment to extract it. The cost
of buying this and bringing it up from the coast was too much
for the miners and many succumbed, as we have seen, to the
lure of Griqualand diamonds (p. 41). Tati became almost a
ghost town, and when Maund saw it in 1885 he noted that it had
a 'deserted and forlorn look', while mining was at a standstill.

Such was the condition of northern Bechuanaland when the
British Government sent the Warren Expedition to rescue the
southern chiefs.

Since the troubles of 1878–9 Warren had been knighted for
his services as leader of the expedition to Arabia in search of the
explorer E. H. Palmer, and it was as a temporary major-general
that he landed at Cape Town in December 1884 as commander
of the Bechuanaland Expedition. His force consisted of four to
five thousand men, part regulars from England, part volunteers
recruited in South Africa. His instructions were to 'remove the
filibusters from Bechuanaland, to restore order in the territory,

to reinstate the natives on their lands, to take such measures as may be necessary to prevent further depredation, and, finally, to hold the country until its further destination is known'.[6]

Almost immediately on landing Warren made the first, indeed perhaps the only mistake of the expedition. He allowed himself to be cozened by the Robinson–Rhodes combine into sending a telegram to van Niekerk endorsing Rhodes's settlement in Stellaland. It was only later that he realized that the settlement included recognition without enquiry of the freebooters' land titles, and he tried to explain his telegram away. But the damage was done, and the last chance of saving Mankurwane's land was destroyed.

Warren marched north and to Robinson's consternation insisted on having Mackenzie with him. But as Rhodes was there as well there was no danger that the General would be allowed to forget that there were two points of view. The arrangement did not however last very long. The differences between Warren and Rhodes became so bitter that the latter severed his connection with the expedition at Vryburg, in a letter that must surely be one of the longest of its kind on record.

At Fourteen Streams Warren met Kruger, who did his best to shield his wayward *protégés* at Rooigrond. He made no impression on Warren, who went on to Stellaland and thence to Mafeking, prepared to deal faithfully with the men of Goshen. But these vanished into the Transvaal at his approach and the object of the expedition was thus accomplished without fighting.

While Warren was making his way to Bechuanaland there were new developments in London. The origins lay in British awareness of German activity in South-West Africa. The settlement founded by Adolf Lüderitz at Angra Pequeña in 1883 was growing into a full-blown German protectorate. Was there not now a danger that the Germans might join hands with hostile Boers or with Portuguese, or even with other Germans who were in East Africa, cut the road to the north and thus

permanently bar the Cape from access to central Africa? The
Scramble for Africa was under way, and on 27 January 1885 an
Order in Council under the Foreign Jurisdiction Acts established
British power and jurisdiction in 'the parts of South Africa
situate west of the . . . South African Republic . . .; north of
the Colony of the Cape of Good Hope; east of the 20th meridian
of east longitude and south of the 22nd parallel of south
latitude; and not within the jurisdiction of any civilized power'.
Germany was informed that the territory so described had been
taken under British protection, and Warren had hardly arrived
in Mafeking when he was instructed to announce the Protectorate to Setshele and Khama, and to see to it that no 'filibustering expedition' take possession of the country, especially
Shoshong.[7]

Warren and Mackenzie set off into northern Bechuanaland to
announce the Protectorate to the chiefs. Khama had asked for
British protection as early as 1876[8] and he accepted the
announcement wholeheartedly, only questioning the northern
boundary, which, he complained, cut his country in half.
Gaseitsiwe made no fuss, but Setshele and his son Sebele were
cagey and suspicious, the latter aggressive. However, they came
round in the end, and all three chiefs offered to surrender to
Britain large tracts of land in their countries for occupation by
English, not Boer, settlers. Warren described the offer as
'magnificent', and incorporated it in the plan for the administration of the Protectorate which he was instructed to prepare.

Warren's plan, which bears Mackenzie's unmistakable im-
print, envisaged a form of Crown Colony government divorced
from the Cape, with magistrates, professional and technical
officers and a police force. For his revenue Warren relied on
customs duties, hut tax, postal charges and especially on rents
from a settlement scheme on the land offered by the chiefs. Any
deficit would be made up by a grant from Great Britain for the
maintenance of the police.

This was just the type of close administration that the British

Government wished to avoid and Downing Street recoiled from
it in horror. 'It would . . . keep us in the interior of South
Africa for ever', wrote the anguished Fairfield. Opportunely the
High Commissioner, who had quarrelled with Warren on almost
every detail of the expedition, had a scheme of his own. This,
after tearing Warren's plan to pieces, he now presented. We
have no interest in the country north of the Molopo, he said,
except as a road to the interior. We should therefore do as little
there in the way of administration as possible, and simply content ourselves with preventing it from being overrun by freebooters and foreigners. The chiefs should continue to govern
their countries in their own way, and their offer of land for
settlement should be refused. Mackenzie's old protectorate
south of the Molopo could not be held much longer with only the
Order in Council of 27 January to go on. This area, said Robinson, should be declared 'British soil', in other words a Crown
Colony, with an administrative and judicial system that would
enable eventual transfer from the Crown to the Cape Colony to
take place more easily. A police force of five hundred men,
falling in the third year to one hundred, would be enough to
protect the country against freebooters; and by the end of the
third year, prophesied Robinson, revenue and expenditure
would 'more nearly' balance each other.[9]

This was what the British Government wanted to hear and
the Robinson plan carried the day. It was now possible to get
rid of Warren, whose activities the Colonial Office had been
watching with increasing anxiety, and the Special Commissioner was recalled in a letter expressing high appreciation of
his services. On 30 September 1885 southern Bechuanaland was
proclaimed to be a British colony under the name of British
Bechuanaland, while the area stretching northwards from the
Molopo river up to latitude 22° remained 'under Her Majesty's
Protection'.

With the proclamation of British Bechuanaland the increasingly shadowy existence of the Stellaland Republic came

definitively to an end, while Goshen, which had in fact slipped away when Warren appeared on the scene, was quietly absorbed into the South African Republic. The freebooters' leader Gey van Pittius is commemorated in a street named after him in Mafeking, the citadel that he and his followers tried so hard to destroy.

Thus was accomplished the division of Bechuanaland west of the Transvaal into two separate political entities, Protectorate and Crown Colony. On 1 October 1885 Mr (later Sir) Sidney Shippard, a judge of the Supreme Court of the Cape Colony, a man of some intellectual distinction and incidentally a good friend of Rhodes, was appointed Administrator of British Bechuanaland and Resident Commissioner for the Protectorate. In both offices Shippard was subordinate to Cape Town. As Governor of the Cape Colony Sir Hercules Robinson was also Governor of British Bechuanaland, while as High Commissioner he virtually governed the Protectorate. The headquarters of the local Administration were at Vryburg.

It is apposite here to add that time justified the Warren plan. If Warren exaggerated the revenue, Robinson very much underestimated the expenditure. His budget was nearly double that of Warren in the first year and his long-range forecast was proved wildly wrong. So far from decreasing, police expenditure rose, at times dramatically, constituting by far the largest item in a budget that was not in sight of equilibrium for years.

Warren's administrative concept was also the more realistic. He did not pretend, as Robinson did, that one can throw an imaginary fence round a vast strategic area and then ignore all that goes on inside. It soon became imperative to set up a modest apparatus of government within the Protectorate, and in this respect the territory in due course came to resemble any other British dependency of the colonial kind.

In an effort to do as much as was still possible to save land for the Tlhaping, Warren before he left obtained one concession from the Colonial Office. Although there could be no going back on Rhodes's wholesale admission of land titles, it was agreed that titles obtained unfairly or by flagrant coercion might be reported on. Warren set up a committee to investigate such cases but its findings were overtaken by the appointment of a land commission soon after Shippard's arrival. The committee's report, however, clearly shows the destitute condition to which the Tlhaping were reduced by the encroachments of the Stellalanders.

When Warren left Mackenzie went with him, and before the end of the year he followed the General to England. He had put his hand to the plough and would not turn aside while he could still 'work for the gradual unifying of South Africa under the Crown, peaceful expansion and territorial government'.[10] Much had been achieved but there was still a danger that 'evil men, and jealous men, and simply stupid men' might undo the good work.[11] Imperial not Colonial government for the whole of Bechuanaland must be assured, and the protectorate must be pushed up to the Zambezi.

VII · The British South Africa Company

Bechuanaland north of the Molopo was taken 'under Her Majesty's protection' because it provided the best way from the Cape into the interior. This does not mean that there was then a bold imperial drive towards the north. On the contrary, the Protectorate remained, as far as the Colonial Office was concerned, a vacuum, an insurance against others getting there first, certainly not a region to be exploited and expanded. The main theme in the history of northern Bechuanaland in the next decade is its development as a line of communication. The impetus came not from London but from Cape Town, and the agency was Colonial not Imperial.

In consonance with its modest role as a passage-way, the Protectorate was undertaken on a basis of minimal responsi-bility. The territory would be defended against 'filibusters and foreign Powers', and for the rest must be left to look after itself. The existence of powerful chiefs and a strong framework of tribal government seemed to make this entirely possible. It was on this basis that the staff was established: a large police force to defend the border and, grudgingly, an administrative officer or two to keep in touch with the chiefs. What more was needed for a corridor?

Several urgent matters engaged the Administrator's atten-tion immediately on his appointment. In British Bechuanaland there was the land question, and this was settled by a commis-sion under Shippard which did less than justice to the Africans.

North of the Molopo the most nagging problem was that of the 'disputed territory'. The territory in question was a strip of land 20 miles wide and 125 miles long between the Motloutse river in the south and the Shashe river in the north. The dispute lay in whether the strip belonged to the Ngwato or to the Matabele. There was plenty of evidence for both claims and either side could establish something of a case.

Both Khama and Lobengula, Mzilikazi's successor as chief of the Matabele, left to themselves would probably have been perfectly content to let the matter lie dormant. But the area was believed to be rich in gold and the question of ownership was kept open and exacerbated by European concession hunters who tried to exploit the chiefs' rival claims to their own advantage. There was for several years a real fear, well founded or otherwise, that the 'disputed territory' might cause a war between the Ngwato and the Matabele. In addition to the danger of tribal war there was also another cause for concern. The area provided the Transvaal with a possible outlet for expansion in the north, a route whereby the Protectorate might be outflanked and neutralized.

The Shashe-Motloutse strip remained a source of anxiety for ten years, though in the event no major conflict arose from it. The question was finally settled in Chamberlain's arbitrament between Khama, Sebele and Bathoen and the British South Africa Company in 1895, when the 'disputed territory' was included in Khama's country for good and all.

It is in the context of this dispute that one must see the astringent attitude of the Administration towards certain Europeans who at the end of 1885 tried to acquire land on or near the Ngwato-Matabele border. The more adventurous of these, forming a body calling itself the Khama Deputation and headed by a former Bechuanaland Border Policeman, were arrested on their way, at Molepolole, brought back, tried and bound over. A second group, the Colonial and British North Bechuanaland Association, made a more formal approach by way of an application to the Colonial Office backed by no less an authority than John Mackenzie. The application was firmly turned down. A third group was more modest: two men apparently out for what they could get from Khama, which they should have known was not very much. They were dealt with in the same way as the Khama Deputation.

In addition to these as it were external anxieties the Tswana themselves had feuds and boundary disputes in which the Administration felt compelled to arbitrate, thereby making hay of the original intention to do as little by way of administration in the Protectorate as possible.

Indeed the policy of non-intervention was an early casualty; and that at the hand of Robinson himself. In May 1886 he wrote a memorandum[1] in which he proposed that the Protectorate should be greatly extended northwards, and that an assistant commissioner should be stationed north of the Molopo. The question of extending the Protectorate was shelved in the Colonial Office, but Robinson's second proposal bore fruit in the appointment of John Moffat, then an assistant magistrate in British Bechuanaland, as Assistant Commissioner in the Protectorate.

From 1859 to 1865 Moffat had laboured at Inyati in Matabeleland; but Livingstone's recall from the Zambezi and his relinquishment of the consular rank which he held there so reduced his resources that he could no longer pay the subsidy that enabled Moffat to be a free-lance. Moffat was therefore compelled to rejoin the London Missionary Society. At the same time his wife's ill health and his own made it necessary for them to reside at Kuruman, where John helped his father during the last years of the latter's ministry in Africa. He stayed on at Kuruman after Robert's retirement in 1870, but he quarrelled with his colleagues Mackenzie and Ashton, and after several uncomfortable years he went to Molepolole in 1877. Continued ill health and disagreements with his colleagues decided him to retire, which he did in 1879.

After leaving the Society Moffat entered government service in the Transvaal which had been annexed by the British in 1877. Soon after the retrocession in 1881 he became a resident magistrate in Basutoland, then under the administration of

the Cape Colony. The Imperial Government took over Basutoland from the Colony in 1884 and made a clean sweep of the
staff. John Moffat went with the rest, but in 1885 came
the timely opening in British Bechuanaland.

Moffat's instructions on taking up his appointment in the
Protectorate were to help the chiefs to repel invasion; to abstain
from interfering with native administration; and to discourage
European settlement. He was to influence the chiefs for good in
the government of their people and advise them in their relations
with their neighbours. Moreover his range was not limited by
the boundaries of the Protectorate. Having visited the Tswana
chiefs he might go on to Bulawayo, the Matabele capital and
make friends with Lobengula. His policy at Lobengula's court
would be to maintain amicable relations with the chief, to
secure the safety of Europeans in the country, and, in Robinson's
words, to 'promote . . . the extension of British influence and
trade throughout Matabeleland and Mashonaland'.

Moffat threw himself enthusiastically into tribal affairs; so
much so indeed that the Colonial Office became worried by the
Assistant Commissioner's tendency to 'protect too much'.[2]
However, important developments in the north soon removed
him from the Protectorate scene and plunged him into the affairs
of Matabeleland, where his activity had lasting consequences.

In spite of the failure of the Tati gold-field, the belief persisted that the region beyond the Limpopo contained enormous
mineral wealth. As European hunters penetrated deeper into
the interior tales came back of old mine workings, relics of
a long-dead gold industry, encouraging the hope that away
in the north, between the Limpopo and the Zambezi, there was
a land of Eldorado waiting to be exploited. This was the ancient
empire of the Mwenemutapa, the legendary monarch or rather
dynasty of monarchs who held sway over east-central Africa
during the period roughly corresponding to the European
middle ages, and whose people were perhaps the original
builders of the great stone city of Zimbabwe.

At the end of 1887 Robinson received news that an envoy of President Kruger named Piet Grobler had been busy at Lobengula's court, and had actually negotiated a treaty giving the South African Republic a footing in Matabeleland. On hearing this the High Commissioner instructed Moffat to go to Bulawayo to counter Kruger's move (Shippard says that Robinson, reluctant at first, was persuaded by Rhodes, who undertook all financial liability³). As son of Mzilikazi's revered friend 'Moshete', and himself a former Matabeleland missionary, Moffat had considerable influence among the Matabele, and in February 1888 he concluded with Lobengula a treaty which confirmed an old friendship and placed the whole foreign policy of the chief in the hands of the British Government. This frustrated any ambitions that the Transvaal may have entertained in Matabeleland. It also prepared the way for the Rudd Concession and ultimately for the colonization of Rhodesia.

The unfortunate Grobler, whose diplomatic *coup* had thus been defeated, died some six months later from a wound received in a clash with a regiment of Khama's men in the 'disputed territory'. Shippard held an enquiry and decided that the wound had been accidentally caused by one of Grobler's own party.⁴

On 30 October 1888 Lobengula gave to three of Rhodes's emissaries, C.D. Rudd, J.R. Maguire and F.R. Thompson, 'complete and exclusive charge over all metals and minerals' in his country, 'together with full power to do all things that they may deem necessary to win and procure the same, and to hold, collect, and enjoy the profits and revenues if any derivable from the said metals and minerals', and to keep all other concession hunters out of the country. In return the concessionaires offered to give Lobengula one hundred pounds a month, one thousand rifles with ammunition, and, of all things, an armed steamboat on the Zambezi river. One year later an amalgamated company purporting to represent all concessionaires with interests in the Bechuanaland Protectorate and in the country north of it was granted a royal charter under the name of British South Africa Company. There was an influential board of directors which included Rhodes, who was in fact the Company's creator and inspiration.

The Company's charter defined the field of operations as 'the region of South Africa lying immediately to the north of British Bechuanaland, and to the north and west of the South African Republic, and to the west of the Portuguese Dominions', thus including the Bechuanaland Protectorate. The Tati area, which in spite of claims by Ngwato chiefs was at that time generally regarded as a dependency of Matabeleland, was expressly excluded. This was because a group calling itself the Tati Concession Mining and Exploration Company was already operating in the area under an exclusive grant from Lobengula.

Within its field the British South Africa Company was authorized to acquire, and, with the approval of the Secretary of State to exercise, powers of any kind whatever 'including powers necessary for the purposes of government, and the preservation of public order'. The Company could make laws, maintain a police force, establish banks, communications and public utilities, and indeed fulfil all the functions of an ordinary colonial government. This was an enormous inflation of the Rudd Concession, that is the grant that Lobengula had made to Rudd and his friends, which referred only to minerals.

John Mackenzie, campaigning in England for an extension of the Bechuanaland Protectorate to the Zambezi under Imperial auspices, saw the British South Africa Company's charter as a tragic mistake. Especially did he condemn the provision whereby the Company might obtain powers of government and administration from African chiefs. Government, he said, was not the proper function of a commercial concern. It was a matter for the best type of British official. The new Company would be no more capable than the Government of the Cape Colony of dealing fairly with African tribesmen. Let the Company stick to trading and mining, said Mackenzie, and leave the task of administration to those qualified to perform it. In the hands of a trading company the opening of Matabeleland would probably be 'more speedy and more violent'.[5]

Mackenzie might have saved his breath. To the British Government the charter was providential, not least the part to which Mackenzie took exception: that enabling the Company to acquire powers of government. It was now possible to secure central Africa, head off troublesome Boers, Germans and Portuguese, arrange an orderly administration in the existing Protectorate, and satisfy a growing appetite for imperial expansion, all with the minimum of official responsibility and without spending a penny of public money. Rhodes and the Company would see to everything. 'The example of the Imperial [British] East African [sic] Company', exulted the Colonial Office, 'shows that such a body [a chartered company] may to some considerable extent relieve Her Majesty's Government from diplomatic difficulties and heavy expenditure. In Lord Knutsford's judgement such a company as that proposed for the Bechuanaland Protectorate, if well conducted, would render still more valuable assistance to Her Majesty's Government in South Africa.'[6] To this may be added that the administrative 'Establishment' in South Africa, Robinson, the High Commissioner, Graham Bower, the Imperial Secretary, and Shippard, the Resident Commissioner, were all heart and soul on Rhodes's side. In England and in South Africa investors eagerly bought shares in the new enterprise.

The financial benefits of the charter became apparent immediately. A telegraph line to Shoshong had figured in the Bechuanaland estimates for 1889–90 but had been turned down by an inexorable Treasury. Rhodes, without waiting for the charter, offered to pay forthwith for a line from Mafeking to Tati, and furthermore to provide the salary of a British representative in Matabeleland. These offers were readily accepted and Moffat agreed to go to Matabeleland as British representative. After some hesitation it was decided to appoint a replacement in the Protectorate. This was W. H. Surmon of the Basutoland Administration, a tactful and efficient man with a reputation for personal courage. It was typical of Treasury attitudes that as a *quid pro quo* for this appointment a much needed water-boring machine had to be dropped from the estimates.

The Protectorate now became the advanced base for Rhodes's occupation of the interior, and all other considerations were henceforward subordinated to that grand design.

The Protectorate chiefs had as yet no idea of the plans that were being made for them and for their people. In 1888, at the time when the British South Africa Company was formed, they were still in the dark as to the real political relationship between the protecting Power and themselves. They understood that a protectorate meant protection not against British concession holders, nor against Germans and Portuguese, nor against each other, but against Boers. For the rest they held to the Colonial Office fiction that the Protectorate was external only, and that they would continue to govern their people in their own way as they had always done.

But this interpretation left open many questions. What for instance was to happen when a chief condemned someone to death for a crime that by civilized standards was not a crime, such as sorcery (even when, as in one case happened, the sentence stipulated that the execution should not take place on Sunday?) [7] Should the Administrator take no action in the event of inter-tribal war? Could pressure be applied to 'protected' tribesmen to pay something towards the cost of the police? Could the chiefs be compelled to co-operate in the establishment of communications, especially towards the north? Administrative attitudes, which seemed to vary with the occasion, did nothing to make the position clearer.

The constitutional position, in so far as it could be said to exist at all, was not one that would be readily grasped by the chiefs, or indeed by any layman. It rested on concessions of power which Warren had received from the chiefs in 1885 under the Foreign Jurisdiction Acts. The concessions varied. Khama had given the Queen authority to make laws in his country both for white and for black. Setshele conceded jurisdiction over white people only. Gaseitsiwe gave the Queen the right to rule 'above' him but reserved the right under her to govern his own people. Lentswe, chief of the Kgatla, was not asked and Moremi away in Ngamiland was never thought of. Jurisdiction under these concessions was therefore fairly full in Khama's country, somewhat less so in Gaseitsiwe's, applicable only to Europeans in Setshele's, and non-existent in Lentswe's and Moremi's. There was also the overriding limitation that the principle of Foreign Jurisdiction was not thought to apply to any but British subjects.

In addition to political problems, the Administration was in economic and financial difficulties. Expenditure was rising and there was no commensurate revenue. Communications were very slow and government-sponsored social services non-existent. Such educational and medical work as there was depended largely on the missionaries. Meanwhile Rhodes's advance into Mashonaland was in the offing, and this would require a reasonable understanding with the Tswana chiefs and some elementary arrangements for transport and communications.

With these considerations in mind Shippard called a grand meeting of chiefs at Kopong in the Kwena country in February 1889, to discuss with them a comprehensive agenda which included defence, taxation, social services and communications, especially a telegraph line. The meeting was a disaster. The chiefs came out strongly against the agenda, especially where it touched on taxation and communications. Although in the event Shippard discarded most of the items, he could make no headway against a defiant opposition. Only Khama and one or two of the lesser tribal leaders were ready to discuss matters in a calm and reasonable way, and Shippard, perhaps wrongly, brought the meeting to an abrupt conclusion with nothing done.[8]

The Colonial Office blamed Shippard for the fiasco but the failure was not really his. The main fault lay in the indeterminate nature of the Protectorate. As long as the chiefs knew that Shippard was powerless to obtain his requirements by force, it was useless to expect them to throw away their independence and to oblige him by raising taxes. The way to enable him to get the facilities he needed was to give him the power to demand them. As it was he went into battle without ammunition.

Once the Company had obtained its charter and was mustering its pioneers to move through the Protectorate into Mashonaland, the telegraph could no longer be delayed, whether the chiefs wanted it or not, and it was duly erected. So also was a fort near the Notwane river close to the town of the Tlokwa chief Gaborone. Thus was founded the station that later became the capital of modern Botswana. A police camp was likewise built on the Motloutse river at the southern edge of the 'disputed territory'. On 11 July 1890 the Company's pioneers began to enter Mashonaland.

Sir Hercules Robinson retired from the post of High Commissioner in 1889. He was a strange man, and not on the whole an attractive one. Graham Bower, his Imperial Secretary, who later sacrificed his career for Robinson, probably describes him as accurately as any: 'Sir Hercules was cold and calculating, very cautious and without any personal ties or personal friendships or hatreds. His first instinct was to secure his safety.' But at the same time, says Bower, Robinson in his prime 'had the clearest head, the best judgement and most balanced mind of any man I ever knew'. A cold fish, but a clever one. Robinson was succeeded by Sir Henry Loch.

It did not take the new High Commissioner long to decide that there must be some more adequate machinery of administration in the Protectorate, and that changing circumstances made its absence ever more intolerable. Non-interference may have been well enough when protection was thought to be only a matter of keeping out foreigners and land-grabbers. But the concept of a mere external protectorate was wilting under the pressure of events. The position of Bechuana-land as a line of communication to the interior, penetration of the country by traders and miners and the interlacing of Euro-pean and African interests, the presence of missionaries and the watchfulness of humanitarian organizations, the proximity of an independent Boer republic and the nomadic propensities of its citizens, the very existence of an Administration to which the chiefs and especially their overmighty subjects could and did appeal – all these made nonsense of the original intention simply to hold the periphery and leave the centre to look after itself. To meet the situation Loch proposed that the territory should be formally annexed and become a Crown Colony, like British Bechuanaland.

This went too far for the Colonial Office. Was it not precisely to avoid the responsibilities that Loch seemed so anxious to incur that a charter was granted to the British South Africa Company? Instead another Order in Council was promulgated, still under the Foreign Jurisdiction Acts, conferring on the High Commissioner power to legislate in the Protectorate. The new Order, which was dated 30 June 1890, was also based on the chiefs' concessions of power, and therefore left the legal position still in doubt. Moreover Loch was told that the only use he should make of it for the moment was to arrange for proper discipline in the Bechuanaland Border Police and in the Company's police. (The difficulty of ensuring discipline in these forces without a suitable code had been a major point in Loch's plea for greater powers.)

The most important aspect of the new Order, however, was the extent of the area over which it applied. This was stated to be 'the parts of Africa situate north of British Bechuanaland; west of the South African Republic and of Matabeleland; east of the German Protectorate; and south of the River Zambezi and not within the jurisdiction of any civilized power'. The northern limit of British jurisdiction was no longer latitude 22°, which in any case was a meaningless boundary. The effect of the Order was to push the Protectorate up to the Zambezi and ultimately to add some 120,000 square miles to the British dominions.

In accordance with Colonial Office instructions Loch legislated only for police discipline, a very small mouse to emerge from such a large mountain. But he still pressed for more, and on 9 May 1891 another Order in Council appeared, a far more comprehensive and detailed instrument than its predecessor. This Order gave the High Commissioner wide powers of legislation, and the power to appoint deputy or resident commissioners, judges, magistrates and other officers, to administer justice, to raise revenue, and generally to provide for 'the peace, order and good government of all persons' within the limits of the Order. Unlike the previous Order, this one extended as far as 'the Portuguese Possessions', thus embracing Matabeleland and Mashonaland, the Company's immediate field of operations.

The times were propitious for a bold step forward. On the one hand international agreements in 1890–1 in the main effected the partition of Africa among the European Powers. On the other, the General Act of the Brussels Conference had encouraged the idea of European administrative activity in African countries as a counter to the slave trade. But the British Government had not intended that Loch should use the wide powers bestowed on him by the Order. These were meant to be kept strictly in reserve, only to be used as a last resort if otherwise insuperable difficulties arose. In the Bechuanaland Protectorate law courts might be set up if this was unavoidable, but the authority of the British Government must be obtained first. In the territory in immediate occupation of the Chartered Company, legislation and administration were the functions of the Company itself. The order was intended simply to support the powers granted by the charter.

The British Government were mistaken in their man. The

Order in itself had no force until it was implemented by local legislation, and this Loch proceeded forthwith to enact. Within a few days of receiving the Order, in fine disregard of his instructions, he published his proclamation of 10 June 1891 which endowed the territories under his authority with a complete system of administration. The proclamation provided for the appointment of resident commissioners, assistant resident commissioners, magistrates and police officers, established courts of law and laid down legal procedure, regulated trade licensing, the sale of arms and ammunition, matters of civil status and the ownership of land. Most important of all, the proclamation made it possible for European courts to hear purely African cases, thus applying the judicial system not only to Europeans but to the whole population.

Unlike Robinson, Loch was not an admirer of the Chartered Company, and he was especially apprehensive of what the Company's officers might do if left to themselves in remote central Africa. In this his views came close to those of John Mackenzie. He believed that legislation should be in the hands of the High Commissioner, while day to day administration in the field should be conducted by imperial officers, paid if necessary by the Company but debarred from taking part in trade. So Loch's proclamation with its commissioners, magistrates, policemen, courts, taxation and licensing was made to cover Mashonaland and Matabeleland no less than the other territories recently brought under the High Commissioner's authority.

The Colonial Office viewed Loch's proclamation with dismay, especially in its application to the Company's territory. The charter had laid the administrative responsibility squarely on the Company and there was no question of superseding it. Loch was compelled to withdraw the administrative provisions in so far as they applied to the Company's immediate field. Those parts relating to the Bechuanaland Protectorate were most reluctantly passed as they appeared to be legally unobjectionable.

The middle of the year 1891 was thus a most significant stage in Protectorate affairs. The Order in Council of 9 May, in spite of the restrictions placed on its use, reflects the recognition by the British Government that the administration of new territories presented problems that the old, casual concept of protectorate could not solve. This Order remained the constitutional foundation of the Protectorate for almost seventy years.

The proclamation of 10 June implementing the Order gave teeth to an Administration hitherto practically powerless and compelled to rely in situations of increasing difficulty on persuasion and argument. These, as Shippard found at Kopong, were by no means always efficacious. The legislation of 1891 made of the Protectorate a type of 'colonial protectorate' in which the Crown possessed and exercised almost complete powers of administration and legislation, differing from true colonies only in legal status.

It is convenient here to follow the Company during the first years in its field of operations. After leaving the Protectorate, Rhodes's pioneers deliberately skirted Matabeleland, possibly on Mackenzie's advice, and went on into Mashonaland. The Matabele were known to be fierce and warlike, whereas the Mashona were believed to be a timid people, grateful to be delivered from Matabele oppression. Having hoisted the flag at Fort Salisbury, the pioneers dispersed, each to stake out his gold claims and his 3000 acre farm.

Whatever Lobengula may have expected from the Rudd Concession, it was certainly not the occupation of country which he considered to be his by two hundred settlers and miners and a strong body of police. Nor can he have foreseen the division of Mashonaland into European farms and the establishment of a European civil administration. Permission to dig for minerals was all that he had granted, yet the fiction that these vastly extended activities were undertaken with Lobengula's authority was maintained, though in reality he objected strongly.

Under these conditions chief and Company could not live happily together for long and matters soon came to a head. After a period of tension war broke out in October 1893, ending in the capture of Bulawayo by the Company's forces, the flight and then the death of Lobengula and the division of his country into farms for the victors.

The Bechuanaland Protectorate was drawn into the war in support of the Company. The police were strongly reinforced and Khama was asked to supply levies, which he did in good measure. The combined force advanced on Matabeleland, beat off one attack by Matabele, and arrived at Bulawayo in the middle of November 1893, nearly a fortnight after the town had been captured by the Company's forces. Khama had removed his contingent some ten days earlier, because, he said, smallpox had broken out among his men and because it was time to begin to plough the land. He may also have become impatient at the leisurely pace of the advance. His withdrawal was criticized by the British authorities, harshly and in retrospect probably unfairly.

The British Government viewed the war with conflicting emotions. It was not pleasant to watch the advance of a British force on the capital of a chief who had been officially described as 'Lobengula our ally'. There was also a suspicion that the incident which had prompted the advance (it had been reported that shots had been fired at a patrol by Matabele) was a put-up job by underlings of the Company. On the other hand there was some apprehension, based on no very obvious grounds, that the Protectorate was in danger of Matabele attack, and there was also an impression that the Company, even though it forced the war, was acting under pressure of circumstances.

Apart from the question of security there were other reasons for official intervention. It was politically impossible for the Government to stand by and see the Company's forces defeated with, perhaps, a consequent massacre of Europeans. But if the Company should win, participation by a British force from the

British Protectorate would give the Government the advantage of a stronger hand, 'a certain controlling and supervising power', in the Company's activities after the war. This was a thing that Loch in particular wanted especially.

The Matabele war justified John Mackenzie's prophecy that the opening of Matabeleland by a mercantile company rather than by an imperial administration would soon lead to violence. At the same time it is difficult to see how any European government, however patient, could have avoided a clash with this despotic society rooted in war. One may however assume that under a normal British colonial government the outcome for the Matabele would have been less disastrous.

Of closer interest now are the long-term consequences of Britain's renouncement of authority in 1889. As Mackenzie with uncanny prescience foresaw, the British Government, by devolving their duties onto a chartered company, did nothing to shift responsibility. If serious difficulties should arise, said Mackenzie, the Government would find that responsibility still rested fairly and squarely on their shoulders. And, as a modern authority has observed, whatever those difficulties may be, the power to remedy them was lost with the charter: 'Britain abandoned the possibility of exercising really effective power in 1889 when she decided against direct administration and conceded this power to a Cape-controlled Chartered Company.'[9]

Nevertheless it must be admitted that the replacement of the Matabele by the Company was something of a relief to the people of Bechuanaland. To the tribes of the north it meant the disappearance of a threat that had hung over them for sixty years. For Khama it removed any possibility of war with the Matabele over the 'disputed territory'. To the Government of the Protectorate it brought a second Assistant Commissioner, for with the establishment of the Company's civil service, Moffat was no longer needed in Bulawayo and in 1892 he came to live at Palapye, the new capital of the Ngwato, who had moved thither in 1889. There were thus two Assistant Commissioners in the Protectorate, Moffat in the north and Surmon in the south.

Incredibly Loch had a struggle to keep them both. On Moffat's return from Matabeleland, the British Treasury, seeing a chance to save money, peremptorily demanded that one of the Assistant Commissioners should go. This meant Surmon, who was only on temporary posting from Basutoland. Loch steeled a hesitant Colonial Office to protest and the situation was ingeniously saved by Fairfield, who persuaded the Treasury to agree to the provisional continuance of both posts. Two years later Surmon's appointment was recognized as permanent.

VIII · Communications and Concessions

The traditional means of transport in Bechuanaland, as in most of southern Africa, was the ox-wagon. It was the vehicle that had brought the Boers into the hinterland at the time of the Great Trek. Formed up in *laager*, that is in a circle with thorn bushes to fill the gaps, ox-wagons also made a fortress, within which the Boers with their firearms had many times held off the attacks of Xhosa, Matabele and other tribes.

The pace of the ox is proverbially slow. Under the best conditions speed was only two or three miles an hour, and not more than twenty miles would be covered in a day. The tracks over which the wagons had to pass were very rough, breakdowns were frequent and the traveller had to be carpenter, wheelwright and blacksmith all in one. The oxen too were a source of anxiety. They were susceptible to extremes of heat and cold, and they needed large quantities of water in a land where water is scarce. The difficulty and expense of moving large bodies of men such as police about Bechuanaland were in themselves enough to persuade the Government to consider seriously any plan for quicker and cheaper transport. In addition postal communications were costly and slow.

During the first years of the Protectorate mails between Shoshong and the outside world were carried by a runner service organized by traders and missionaries through Zeerust in the western Transvaal. This in due course proving inadequate, arrangements were made with various contractors for the carriage of mails by horse- or mule-drawn carts. This service was efficient within its limits, but when the settlement of Mashonaland and Matabeleland began in earnest, a railway became a necessity.

Two companies with an interest in the northern territories approached the Colonial Office on the subject in 1888–9. These were the Bechuanaland Exploration Company and the Exploring Company. Both were directed by the same two men and both threw in their lot with the British South Africa Company when the latter set itself to amalgamate all the various concerns which had interests in Rhodes's future empire. Then in 1892 Rhodes's associate Alfred Beit offered to form a new company, a subsidiary of the British South Africa Company of course, one that would build a railway from Vryburg to Palapye in return for a substantial subsidy from the Government and a lesser one from the parent company and the Tati Company. The railway company would also be endowed with a large block of land in British Bechuanaland.

At the end of 1892 Loch and Rhodes went to England personally to press the railway on the Colonial Office. The result of their mission was the 'Railway Despatch', a monumental document in which the Secretary of State approved the railway proposals and also gave several privileges to the British South Africa Company in addition to the inducements offered to the subsidiary. Local officials were instructed to use their best endeavours to persuade chiefs and people to grant concessions to the Company. The High Commissioner was to make a strict investigation into all claims by other people to concessions in the Protectorate. No claims in respect of concessions made after the date of the charter were to be recognized. These conditions led to the setting up of a Concessions Commission whose activities will be described later.

The Company set to work with the energy characteristic of all Rhodes's enterprises, and the Vryburg–Mafeking section of the railway was opened to traffic in early October 1894. The line was completed to Bulawayo by the end of 1897, the last 400 miles being built within 400 days.

Following roughly the route taken by Rhodes's Pioneers, the telegraph line had reached Salisbury in 1892.

Loch's proclamation of 10 June 1891 provided the Protectorate with reasonably effective machinery of government, and the new concept of protection is reflected henceforward in a more confident approach to domestic problems. The emphasis was now on a stronger line, and this bore particularly hard on Sebele, chief of the Kwena after Setshele's death in 1892. Sebele was restive under any form of control and he came into conflict with the Administration in several incidents shortly after his accession, not least, as we shall see, in matters connected with the Concessions Commission of 1893.

In the north Khama's accession to the chiefship after years of strife within the family and tribe had left many unhealed wounds. Kgamane, Khama's brother, had long been in open opposition and was at the head of a cell of disaffection on the Transvaal side of the Limpopo river. Nearer home, conservative elements still clung to the Sekgoma tradition and resented Khama's wholesale abolition of ancient customs. After the move of the tribal capital from Shoshong to Palapye dissensions became almost continuous, involving several royal headmen and ultimately Khama's son Sekgoma.

In 1892 Khama parted with his missionary J. D. Hepburn, a saintly if emotional man who had served the tribe faithfully for twenty years. Overworked as a result of the Ngwato move from Shoshong to Palapye, his health undermined by malaria, Hepburn allowed his zeal to outrun his discretion and he mortally offended the chief over church matters. When he precipitately removed himself from Palapye, after announcing that he would have no more to do with the Ngwato, Khama took him at his word and refused to have him back.

Discord in the chief's family came to a head in 1895 when a bitter quarrel broke out between Khama and several of his relations, of whom Rraditladi, a brother, was the most important. This too seems to have been connected with church matters, though the actual causes are obscure. There were also accusations of 'attempted sedition', whatever that may mean, 'but', wrote Moffat, who was then Assistant Commissioner at Palapye, 'these charges are singularly misty and have not been dealt with by any calm judicial tribunal'.[1]

Unhappily the dispute caused a breach between Khama and Moffat which, since they were both men of strong character, became irreparable. The Rraditladi party complained to Moffat that Khama harassed them and generally made their lives intolerable. Khama for his part was furious with Moffat for listening to the malcontents and for not siding immediately with him. Moffat, who had been brought up to believe that as an administrator he must keep an open mind on every question even when it concerned the chief, recommended official intervention. Khama agreed that the Government should intervene, but demanded that Moffat should be moved from Palapye, whereupon Shippard held an enquiry and proposed that the discontented relatives should be settled in an area bounded by the watershed of the Motloutse and Mpakwe rivers. Here they would be independent of Khama who should withdraw his cattle posts and give the area to the seceding faction.[2]

This was more than Khama could bear and he played his master stroke: he abolished the ban on making beer, thus violating the principles of a lifetime. The Rraditladi party promptly dwindled dramatically to a number manifestly too small for the space in which Shippard proposed to put them. At this point Rhodes's close friend Dr Jameson came along like a *deus ex machina* and offered to provide the dissidents with land in the British South Africa Company's territory, of which he was then Administrator. There after some delay they went, while Moffat was moved from Palapye to be resident magistrate at Taung in British Bechuanaland.

It will be remembered that the British Government, when approving the railway proposals, had also undertaken to clear the way for the Company in the Protectorate by taking a close look at concessions claimed by other people. In fulfilment of this pledge a commission was set up in 1893 under Surmon's chairmanship. The members were J. Vintcent, Crown Prosecutor, and Major F. W. Panzera. The commissioners began work in May 1893.

A concession was an agreement whereby a chief would give rights of various kinds, which almost always included mineral rights, in return for a consideration. Chiefs usually treated the revenue from concessions as personal income. The system was wide open to abuse and was often shamelessly manipulated by seedy adventurers who worked on the chiefs' vanity and cupidity to obtain valuable benefits for incommensurately small payments. It is well described by Harry Johnston, who must have seen it in operation often enough: 'You get a concession, that is to say you draw up a deed conferring on you all sorts of rights and privileges, you give the chief a rifle, a double-barrelled shot-gun, a musical box, a military uniform with epaulettes, two or three dozen bottles of rum, some red blankets and beads; he makes a cross on your document; and you have it witnessed by a trader or some one. Then you come home and put it on the market.'[3] The system in Bechuanaland was more sophisticated, but the Tswana chiefs still had little idea of what they were giving away or of what they were getting in return.

The Commission investigated forty-five claims, of which some were preposterous beyond belief. For instance in 1890 Setshele, after ratifying certain other grants, conferred on a company calling itself the 'Secheleland Concessions Syndicate' the right for a period of fifty years 'to make ordinances, establish courts of justice, establish and maintain a force of police, regulate the traffic in intoxicating liquors and suppress slavery, to fix and establish tariffs and charges and to remove officials, officers and other servants; the grantee to have the right at the end of fifty years, on payment of £2000, to renew the concession on the same terms for a further period of fifty years'. The same chief gave another concern a lease of 800 square miles, part of which was in the country of another chief, for £200 a year. For sheer impudence the first place must go to the two men who claimed from Montshiwa a farm awarded to 'volunteers' who had fought *against* Montshiwa in the old filibustering days. This claim had already been turned down by the Bechuanaland Land Commission.

Surmon and his colleagues availed themselves of their wide terms of reference to disallow the greater number of claims, thereby doing considerable service to the people of the Protectorate. Their work might have yielded even better results if their terms of reference had been wider; or if the Colonial Office had not seen fit to water down some of their recommendations.

Nevertheless the Commission represents probably the most positive single act of the local British administration in the first decade of the Protectorate's life. Its effect was to eliminate a number of parasites before they had taken good hold on the country; and a true estimate of its achievement may be formed if we consider the case of Swaziland, where wholesale concessions and a too narrow review of them combined to rob the Swazi of a large part of their land.

Valuable as the work of the Commission was, it was not appreciated by all the Tswana chiefs. Sebele's attitude especially was awkward and resentful. He and his father between them had made several scandalous concessions, evidently without understanding what the transaction implied and usually without consulting the tribe in the normal African way. In a protest submitted to the Commission Sebele now claimed that as 'Sovereign of the Soil' he had the right to give grants to whomsoever he pleased without being questioned by anyone. Lentswe put in a similar protest. The Commissioners did no more than record the chiefs' protests before proceeding to business.

To the chiefs the abrogation of concessions meant a loss of income, and several courses were suggested to compensate them. Eventually the ever-handy Rhodes, who by this time had become well used to shouldering responsibilities that would normally be borne by a government, declared himself, that is the Chartered Company, willing to take on the payment of a subsidy to the chiefs. It is difficult to resist the conclusion that men who had so lightly traded away tribal assets were lucky to get anything.

Of all the concessions in the Protectorate the oldest was the Tati, which lies between the Shashe and the Ramokgwebana rivers, and is estimated to have an area of 2069 square miles. In 1880 Lobengula gave to a group calling itself the Northern Light Company the exclusive right to 'seek and dig for gold' in the area. In 1882 this concession was made more comprehensive and in 1887 the chief gave to the trader-pioneer Samuel Edwards powers of government in the district. In 1888 the concession was acquired by the Tati Concession Mining and Exploration Company, and Edwards, as representative of that company, obtained from Lobengula the right to keep other people out of the area. The Rudd Concession and the British South Africa Company's charter both specifically exclude the Tati from their scope.

Hitherto the Tati had been recognized as part of Matabeleland, but a proclamation by Loch on 27 September 1892 placed the district unequivocally in the Bechuanaland Protectorate. Bungling in the Colonial Office went a long way to change Lobengula's limited grant into full ownership and Proclamation 2 of 1911 later confirmed the Tati Company 'in the full, free and undisturbed possession as owners of all the land' in the district.[4]

Concession hunters had pushed even as far as Ngamiland. In 1888, the Tawana ruler Moremi, apparently an amiable and complaisant personality, gave to Messrs Strombom and Nicholls a prospecting right over 400 square miles of his territory. In the following year the chief gave to the same two men, together with another named Hicks, the right to prospect for minerals throughout Ngamiland. This right Nicholls and Hicks (Strombom having died) sold to the British West Charterland Company, and the outcome was the bizarre episode in the life of

Frederick Lugard when in 1896–7 he led an expedition to Ngamiland on behalf of that company to look for gold and diamonds.[5]

At this time officialdom both in England and in Africa was still fairly ignorant about Ngamiland, although a not inconsiderable literature had grown up around the region since it was first visited by Europeans. The Anglo-German treaty of 1890 specifically included Lake Ngami within the British sphere, and Loch's proclamation of 27 September 1892 made Ngamiland part of the Protectorate, though the terms of the proclamation were very vague. To the Colonial Office in 1894 this was still a 'dreadful and distant place' and one for which responsibility should be passed to the Chartered Company without delay.[6]

At the end of 1893 the Company sent a man named Bosman as agent to Ngamiland. Bosman obtained two most comprehensive concessions from Sekgoma, another son of Letsholathebe, who had become chief when Moremi died in 1891. These grants, however, were found to be bogus and were disallowed by the Secretary of State in London. This was particularly embarrassing as the Boer farmers whom Rhodes proposed to plant in Ngamiland were already assembling in the vicinity of Mafeking in preparation for their trek across the Kgalagadi.

It so happened that the idea of establishing a small European community in the north-west was not altogether unwelcome to the British Government. There had been conflict between the Tawana and a neighbouring tribe in German territory. A buffer settlement between Lake Ngami and German South-West Africa might be useful not only to prevent the tribes from causing international complications but also to provide an obstruction to German expansion towards the Transvaal. A pioneering party of Boers was sent off to Ngamiland with a police escort under Captain Fuller to spy out the land. Fuller was to use his best endeavours to induce Sekgoma to grant a new concession to the Company.

This Sekgoma point-blank refused to do. 'We have no desire

to have any agreement with Mr. Rhodes', he declared, 'or to have any friendship with him.' In vain did Fuller try to bring him round. The chief was adamant. He had understood very well the lesson of Matabeleland.

A solution to the difficulty was then discovered. Away to the south-west of Lake Ngami lay Ghanzi, a great expanse suitable for European settlement and occupied only by roving Bushmen. It was *nullius terra* and the only claim to it that the Tawana could set up was that they raided there for slaves. No concession from Sekgoma was therefore necessary, and the British Government could dispose of the area as they chose.

For a number of reasons, including the Jameson Raid at the end of 1895, there was a long delay before this ingenious solution could be worked out in practice. It was not until May 1898 that the prospective settlers, who had been waiting at Maritsani, south of Mafeking, at last set out on their journey. Numbers had dwindled, and only thirty-six families eventually reached Ghanzi, compared to the sixty which had so hopefully assembled in 1894[7].

There is in Botswana a form of land tenure having something of the nature of a concession and it is therefore not out of place to describe it in this context. In 1885 chief Montshiwa, hoping to preserve his country from seizure by Europeans, proposed to give farms in individual tenure to his sons and to other important members of the tribe. Neither the High Commissioner nor, later, the British Bechuanaland Land Commission approved a system giving rights in land to individuals, but in 1892 Montshiwa raised the question again in connection with Rolong land in the Protectorate. This time the High Commissioner, with the approval of the Secretary of State, agreed to a form of alienation which did not amount to freehold but to a right of occupation under conditions, the most important of which was that title might not be transferred in any way except to another Rolong. Montshiwa's country north of the Molopo was divided into forty-one farms of 6000 acres each, and these so-called Barolong Farms were then distributed to individual notables. The rest of the tribe continued to live on the land, but as tenants of the grantees. These 'tenants' enjoy the same land rights as people in any other part of Botswana.[8]

IX · Three Chiefs Call on Mr Chamberlain

The charter of the British South Africa Company clearly and purposefully envisaged that powers of administration in countries within its field of operations would be assumed by the Company. In practice there was some confusion as to how these powers could be obtained. The charter provided that powers of government might be acquired from African chiefs. At the same time there was a tendency, when the question of Bechuanaland came up, to regard transfer of power to the Company as a thing that could be done as an act of government.

The only precedent was not a reassuring one. The Rudd Concession was nothing more than a mineral concession. With this the Chartered Company had occupied Mashonaland with pioneers and police, driven Lobengula to exile and death, and established a government of its own in Matabeleland.

Until 1894 the Company was too absorbed in Rhodesia to worry about Bechuanaland, but at the end of that year Rhodes formally applied for an assurance that the Government would in due course transfer the administration of the Protectorate to the Company, 'thus carrying out the terms of the charter and the former assurances of their predecessors'.[1] The Secretary of State, Lord Ripon, replied at once that the Government, 'when the time comes', would consider any reasonable proposals for transfer.

The Tswana meanwhile had got wind of what was going on. In July 1895 Khama, Bathoen, Sebele and Lentswe sent petitions to the new Colonial Secretary, Joseph Chamberlain, praying that their countries should not be handed over to the Company and that they and their people should continue to be protected by the Queen. Khama, Sebele and Bathoen, accompanied by the missionary W. C. Willoughby, then left for England to protest in person to the Secretary of State.

The chiefs found Mr Chamberlain in a cautious mood. He referred to the promises of his predecessors, by which he felt himself bound. By placing themselves under the Company, he said, the chiefs would still be under the Queen, since the Company was bound to obey the Queen's directions. (Remembering the fate of Lobengula, the chiefs can have got small comfort from this.) He advised the chiefs to come to terms with the Company and he himself would try to settle any differences. Mr Chamberlain then went on holiday.

The chiefs went back to their hotel and 'put their words on paper' by the hand of Willoughby. 'There is no government', they said, 'that we can trust like that of the Great Queen.' They feared the Chartered Company 'because we fear that they will take our land and sell it to others. . . . We fear that they will fill our country with liquor shops.' They had no faith in a mere agreement to protect them once they had fallen under Company rule, for, they said, 'we have no voice that can be heard in England'. Let Mr Chamberlain appoint one of his own people to live among them, 'a good man who knows our speech and customs, who is not bad-tempered and impatient, one who loves us'. Let this man, said the chiefs, be Mr Chamberlain's eyes and ears and 'become also our mouth, which shall speak our words to you'.

The only reply from the Colonial Office to this eloquent and moving document was an abrupt résumé of the chiefs' first interview with the Colonial Secretary and renewed advice to come to terms with the Company. As to the appointment of a Resident, this would be dealt with on Mr Chamberlain's return from holiday.

The chiefs put the time of waiting to good use. Under the auspices of the London Missionary Society, whose centenary it was, and accompanied by the vigilant Willoughby, they set out on a tour of the country. In an orgy of sightseeing, religious meetings and receptions, the chiefs put their case to the British public. Although the Colonial Office watched these junketings with sour disapproval, the press was enthusiastic, and a significant body of public opinion distinctly sympathetic, especially to Khama, that 'pious and abstinent sovereign',[2] whose name was well known in England.

'The missionary feeling in England', wrote the *Sunday Times*, 'is immensely strong, its tendency to grow and no British Ministry can ignore its political influence.'[3] It was an influence to which Chamberlain might be particularly susceptible. He had old connections with John Mackenzie, whom he first met through the eminent nonconformist divine Dr Dale, Chamberlain's associate in the reform of local government in Birmingham. Chamberlain was also a member of Mackenzie's South African Committee and had been a firm advocate of British intervention to save the southern Tswana chiefs from the Boers. His influence in this matter among his Cabinet colleagues was decisive, and he spoke forcibly for the Warren Expedition in the House of Commons. Finally, all his instincts were in favour of imperial rule and against the delegation of colonial responsibilities to other agencies.

Even so, to anyone who had merely read the chiefs' petitions and the Colonial Office's disheartening replies, the proceedings of the meeting which took place on 6 November on Chamberlain's return from holiday come as a surprise. The chiefs got all they wanted, and perhaps a little more than they expected. The extensive claims made to Warren were considerably scaled down, but the areas allotted to each chief were still very large. The reserves, as they were henceforward called, followed the existing tribal boundaries so far as they were known, less a strip for the railway, which they were quite willing to concede. Within their reserves the chiefs would remain under the Queen's protection and would continue to rule their people 'much as at present'. The Queen would appoint a Resident, and the people would pay a tax, which the chiefs would collect.

Strong drink would not be allowed into the country and there would be a small African police force of men 'not addicted to strong drink'. The country outside the reserves allocated to the chiefs would be administered by the Chartered Company.[4]

Chamberlain's arbitrament was a signal defeat for Rhodes, who expressed his rage in furious telegrams to his agent in London. But the chiefs had won, and the Company, so it appeared at the time, was now left with only a vast expanse of wasteland. Even this consolation prize was one that Rhodes was not able to enjoy, for it vanished with a cataclysmic event that soon shook the whole of southern Africa.

While Khama and his fellow chiefs were touring England and discussing their future with the Colonial Secretary, there had been ominous activity in Bechuanaland. In September 1895 Rhodes told the High Commissioner that he proposed to apply to chief Ikaneng of the Lete for his assent to the transfer of his country to the Company's administration. The High Commissioner was once more Rhodes's old friend Sir Hercules Robinson, who had been appointed for a second term. Rhodes's approach, fully endorsed by Robinson, was curiously timed, as the Colonial Office did not fail to notice. On the one hand negotiations were just about to begin in London with chiefs Khama, Sebele and Bathoen. On the other it was assumed that the Lete and their chief were not independent, but subordinate to Bathoen. However, Rhodes's negotiations with Ikaneng were allowed to proceed, provided that Robinson was satisfied that Bathoen's consent to the transaction was not necessary.

Fortified by advice from Robinson as to how pressure might best be applied on the chief, Shippard proceeded to Ramotswa, together with Cecil Rhodes's brother Frank, the Company's emissary, and interviewed Ikaneng. In spite of previous assumptions to the contrary, he had no difficulty in discovering that the Lete were independent of the Ngwaketse, and therefore quite capable of surrendering themselves to the Company without reference to Bathoen. But he also found Ikaneng strangely attached to the existing dispensation and reluctant to change. However the chief came round in the end, almost certainly under the impression that he was merely granting a site for a temporary magistracy during the construction of the railway.

From Ramotswa Shippard came back south to see Montshiwa, whom with the same ease he persuaded to 'acquiesce' in the administration by the Company of his country in the Protectorate. The name of the place offered by the chief as a site for a camp was Pitsanaphotlokwe, about three miles from the Transvaal border.

In reporting the capitulation of Ikaneng and Montshiwa Robinson suggested that it would be better to take advantage of the offers of land made to Warren in 1885 and transfer to the Company the whole of the country on the Transvaal border traversed by the first section of the railway.

The Colonial Office already suspected that Shippard's methods with Ikaneng and Montshiwa had been disingenuous, and Robinson's new approach drew out a mild but unmistakable rebuke. The chiefs' offer of land in 1885, said Mr Chamberlain, had been turned down on Robinson's own advice and it could not be exploited now. But Chamberlain agreed that the countries of Ikaneng and Montshiwa could be ceded to the Company. This was effected by Proclamation 10 of 1895, and Dr Jameson became Resident Commissioner of the ceded territory.

The tragi-comedy of the Jameson Raid has been told many times and there is no need to repeat it in detail here. On the night of 29–30 December 1895, Dr Jameson invaded the Transvaal at the head of 500 fighting men to support an armed rising of *Uitlanders* in Johannesburg against the Government of President Kruger. The *Uitlanders* failed to rise, Jameson and his men were surrounded by the Boers at Doornkop and were compelled ignominiously to surrender.

The Raid has more to do with the history of South Africa than with that of Bechuanaland, but the Protectorate was involved in several ways. First, the expedition started from Pitsanaphotlokwe, the very place that Montshiwa had so conveniently been persuaded to offer to the Company for a camp.

Secondly, many of Jameson's men were former members of the Bechuanaland Border Police. When British Bechuanaland was annexed to the Cape Colony the force was reduced and Rhodes offered to take over the men so discharged. There were further reductions following on Chamberlain's settlement with the chiefs in London. Rhodes's offer appeared to provide a sensible solution to a small unemployment problem and the whole force was moved to Mafeking in order to enable Jameson to decide how many of those wishing to transfer he would be willing to take over. Meanwhile the Company's police were brought down to Pitsanaphotlokwe from the north, thus denuding Rhodesia of security forces. On the night that Jameson started from his base in the Protectorate the men who had engaged with the Company set out from Mafeking and joined the ill-fated expedition at Malmani.

Finally, the Raid caused the collapse of Rhodes's plans for administering the Protectorate. The proclamation ceding the countries of Ikaneng and Montshiwa to the Company was revoked and nothing more was heard about a take-over of Lentswe's country, which was next on the list. Administration by the Company of land outside the reserves was postponed indefinitely. Eight months later, when the Company raised the question, it received a frosty reply.

In accordance with the arrangements made in London, Major H. J. Goold-Adams was given the task of demarcating the Ngwato, Kwena and Ngwaketse reserves, and also reserves for the Tawana and the Kgatla. He had hardly begun when he was ordered on special duty to Barotseland, but his work was continued by C. St Quintin and in Ngamiland by Panzera. The result was Proclamation 9 of 1899 which defined in detail the boundaries of the five reserves. Considering the enormous scope of the work it was a remarkable achievement.

The question of the Company's rights in land was subsequently revived in connection with the titles for the Ghanzi farms (see p. 105). At a meeting with Rhodes in November 1897, the High Commissioner, Lord Milner, conceded that the undertaking to transfer the administration of unallotted land to the Company still subsisted. 'It is in this connection noteworthy', says Lord Hailey,

> that the Southern Rhodesia Order in Council of 1898 reproduced the clause of the Matabeleland Order in Council . . . by virtue of which the Secretary of State was empowered to include the Protectorate within the jurisdiction of the Chartered Company. The Company was never afterwards in a position to press for the exercise of the powers which this provision conferred on the Secretary of State, but from the legal standpoint its rights presumably remained alive until the termination of its Charter in 1923.[5]

In 1904 the Bechuanaland Protectorate (Lands) Order in Council vested in the High Commissioner as Crown Lands the strip ceded by chiefs Khama, Sebele and Bathoen in 1895 for the railway. In the following year this was granted to the British South Africa Company and so were created the so-called Gaberones (Gaborone), Lobatse and Tuli blocks. With the Tati District and Ghanzi, these constitute the areas of European settlement.

In 1910 another Order in Council declared as Crown Lands all the other land in the Protectorate except the reserves, land already subject to a grant, the Tati district and the Barolong Farms.

The boundaries of the Lete reserve, which was contiguous to the Chartered Company's railway strip, were proclaimed in detail in 1909, while the Tlokwa, owing to special circumstances, did not have a reserve of their own until 1933, when they became the beneficiaries of a deal between the Government, the Ngwato and the Company (see p. 131).

X · Pestilence and Famine — Domestic Issues — The Question of Transfer

The last two months of 1895 marked the end of an era in the history of the Bechuanaland Protectorate. British Bechuanaland was at long last incorporated in the Cape Colony, much against the will of the African people but in fulfilment of a policy to which the British Government had always tenaciously adhered. Shippard retired, to be replaced by F. J. Newton, himself alas! destined soon to become a scapegoat for the Jameson Raid.* Following on the transfer of British Bechuanaland to the Cape, the seat of Protectorate government was moved to Mafeking, where it was established on a property magnificently called the Imperial Reserve.

By 1895 the outline of the Protectorate was roughly the same as that of Botswana today. The boundaries of the chiefships within it were still uncertain, and several years were to pass before these were definitely settled. As to European settlement, the Tati Company was in occupation of the Tati area, though its rights vis-à-vis local Africans continued to be debated for a long time; the Ghanzi area was still the haunt of nomadic Bushmen, though Rhodes was already staking his claim to it; and the land along the railway that later became the Lobatse, Gaberones and Tuli blocks had not yet been ceded to the Company.

Politically Chamberlain's arbitrament in London had ended

---

* Newton knew about Jameson's preparations but kept quiet about them, apparently believing that this was what was expected of him. He was sent to an unattractive post in the West Indies but later gave distinguished service to Southern Rhodesia. Graham Bower, the Imperial Secretary, was the other scapegoat.

prevailing uncertainties as to the future of the countries of the three great Tswana chiefs; and the Jameson Raid placed the rest of the Protectorate, in the event permanently, out of the reach of the British South Africa Company.

The first year in the life of the new, or rather renewed Protectorate was made memorable by the visitation of 'an almost unknown disease in its most virulent form, which took for its victims the staple product, the chief means of livelihood, an important item of the food supply, and the capital and the currency of the country'.[1] This was rinderpest, which came southwards at a rate of twenty-five miles a day and destroyed not less than ninety per cent of the cattle of the country. To crown this catastrophe, there was a drought and an invasion of locusts.

The effect of these disasters was not as great as might have been expected, for several reasons. One was that the people were able to make biltong from healthy cattle and, less safely, from diseased ones. Secondly, reserves of cash and of produce were surprisingly large. The Government imported considerable quantities of maize, which was sold at cost price, though some was distributed free to those especially in want. The building of the railway provided paid employment for those who needed it and the Administration also instituted small relief works. There was an increase in the numbers going to work in South Africa.

The most remarkable thing about the situation was the calm and discipline of the Tswana throughout their period of trial. Anti-rinderpest measures, including the destruction of over ten thousand cattle, were carried out by a handful of police, with hardly a murmur of protest from the people. The famine was endured with equal stoicism. This self-restraint in the face of adversity speaks well for the influence of the leaders as well as for the character of the tribesmen, and it is perhaps also a tribute to the good relations existing between the Tswana and the British Administration. In contrast, the natural disasters of 1896 were an important cause of the Matabele Rebellion, while in British Bechuanaland, so recently turned over to the Cape Colony, the shooting of seventeen stray cattle as a prophylactic measure triggered off a rising among the Tlhaping.*

Nevertheless the process of adaptation to British administration in the Protectorate was by no means a painless one. Much of the trouble lay in differing concepts of 'protection'. The chiefs envisaged 'a form of parallel rule, in which they would administer the internal affairs of the tribes without interference from the Administration',[2] and in this they found encouragement in Mr Chamberlain's undertaking that within broad limits they would continue to rule their own people 'much as at present'.†

If the chiefs expected that they would henceforward administer their people under a slightly modified system of Home Rule, they were to be disappointed. The doctrine of non-intervention in tribal matters had been badly breached in the course of years: by Loch's legislation of 1891, by the Concessions Commission of 1893, by the various arrangements to which the chiefs agreed during their interviews with Chamberlain in London. The Resident Commissioner had arbitrated in several dynastic quarrels and boundary disputes. A recalcitrant chief had been fined. Limits had been placed on the jurisdiction of the tribal courts. Although tampering with traditional authority had been kept to a minimum and the Administration was reluctant and slow to interfere in tribal affairs (Shippard was still giving lip-service to non-intervention in 1894),[3] nevertheless Chamberlain's 'much as at present' implied considerable restrictions on the chiefs' freedom of action.

'The fact is', said Loch in 1890, 'that the declaration of the

* The Langeberg Rebellion.
† This is the phrase used in the Colonial Office letter to the chiefs. In a telegram to Robinson the words used are 'as heretofore'. The chiefs' powers were limited by the reservation to the Resident Commissioner of cases involving white men and natives of other tribes or in which the punishment was death, and by a right of appeal to the Resident Commissioner in other serious cases.

Protectorate did impair the sovereign rights of the chiefs and they have from the first been at various times restrained from doing things which had they been free and independent sovereigns they would have been at liberty to accomplish.'[4]

Khama had shown his dislike of official intervention during the Rraditladi affair in 1895 if not before,[5] and Sebele had made his opinions plain at the time of the Concessions Commission in 1893, and also on other occasions. On his return from England in 1895 Khama settled back without difficulty to life with the tenuous British Administration, which was now a permanency. But he retained very clearly in mind Chamberlain's assurance regarding the position of the chief in tribal government, and this became the touchstone on which he judged administrative conduct towards himself and the tribe. 'When I was in England', he wrote many years later, 'Mr Chamberlain gave us the power to exercise our laws and customs.'[6] In several brushes with officialdom during the rest of his long reign he showed himself very sensitive to any measure that appeared to diminish his status or threaten the traditional ties that bound chief and people.

Matters did not proceed so easily with Sebele. The demarcation of the Kwena–Kgatla boundary re-opened an old wound but Sebele's protests made no impression either on the local Administration or on the Secretary of State. The chief had no cause for complaint, however, in the attitude of the Administration towards a quarrel with his brother Kgari and others which arose in 1894 and did not reach its remote conclusion until 1920, after both Sebele and Kgari were dead. In this case the Resident Commissioner supported the chief, not without strong misgivings, in order to save tribal unity.

Of many domestic issues arising during the years following the London settlement, three stand out as of special importance.

The first was the quarrel between Khama and his son and heir Sekgoma. This had been brewing for a long time, and its origins probably lay in domestic differences within the chief's family circle.[7] It was fanned by Rratshosa, Khama's secretary and confidant, between whom and Sekgoma there was much ill-feeling. The quarrel flared up in 1898, and Sekgoma and his followers, who numbered about 2000, went first to Lephepe until 1907, then to Nekati on the Makgadikgadi. In 1916 Sekgoma, hearing that Khama had had an accident, went to Serowe and there was at last a reconciliation between father and son.

In Ngamiland the Tawana were bedevilled for several years by a dynastic dispute between Sekgoma Letsholathebe, the manner of whose succession had been most unusual,[8] and his nephew Mathiba. In contrast to his easy-going predecessor Moremi, Sekgoma was a harsh man, and he alienated the Tawana headmen. They resolved to get rid of him and replace him with Mathiba, who by strict tribal law was indeed the rightful chief.

The headmen obtained the support of Khama whom Sekgoma had deeply offended in connection with a family marriage, and with whom, moreover, he was at odds about the tribal boundary. Meanwhile Sekgoma and Mathiba had learnt that each wished to murder the other, and the latter fled to Khama for sanctuary. By this time most of the leading members of the tribe supported Mathiba, and with Khama as ally the headmen laid their case before the Protectorate Government. In 1906, to avoid bloodshed, Sekgoma was removed to Gaborone and after an enquiry by the Resident Commissioner, Mathiba was made chief, apparently by the almost unanimous wish of the tribe.

This was not the end of the affair. Sekgoma was regarded as dangerous, and it was decided to restrict his movements. Indeed it was at one time actually suggested that he should be exiled from Bechuanaland altogether. An attempt was made on his behalf to obtain a writ of *habeas corpus* for him in the English Courts, but this was unsuccessful. In 1912, after several years of uncertainty, he was allowed to live with his not inconsider-

able following on Crown Land near the Chobe river, where he
died in 1914.

The Mothowagae secession among the Ngwaketse is mentioned here because it was peculiar in having a religious and not
a political origin. Mothowagae Motlogelwa was an evangelist
and teacher of the London Missionary Society who was dis-
missed from his offices by the missionary Edwin Lloyd at
Kanye, allegedly for disobedience. He seceded from the Society
in 1902 taking with him part of his congregation, and founded
a new Church called the 'King Edward Free Bangwaketse
Church'. Chief Bathoen treated the schismatics very carefully
as they included important people, but he fell out with Mothowagae in 1903 and ordered him to leave the reserve, a sentence
that was reduced to banishment to another part of the reserve.
Mothowagae apologized and there was a temporary reconciliation. Later, however, the movement took on a political com-
plexion and just before his death in 1910 Bathoen attempted to
suppress it. Bathoen's successor Seepapitso banished Mothowagae from the chiefdom, and the dissident evangelist went to
Taung in British Bechuanaland.

The South African War of 1899–1902 hardly touched African
life in the Protectorate. The chiefs in all three High Commission
Territories had been told that the war was no concern of theirs
and it was only on the eastern side that the effects of the struggle
were felt at all. Goold-Adams, the Resident Commissioner, was
besieged in Mafeking, and the senior of the two Assistant Commissioners, Surmon at Gaborone, acted for him in the Protectorate. An armoured train with Rhodesian volunteers patrolled
parts of the railway, police scouts kept an eye on Boer detachments in the Transvaal, enemy patrols from time to time dashed
into the Protectorate, and there was occasional shelling across
the frontier. None of this did much harm, though the British
were compelled temporarily to evacuate Gaborone and withdraw northwards.

The only engagement worthy of the name was a muddled and

inconclusive advance on Derdepoort on the Transvaal side of
the Marico river by Rhodesian forces accompanied by Kgatla
auxiliaries. The military results were nil and the consequences
were unfortunate: Boer reprisals on the Kgatla prompted the
latter to raid the Transvaal, lifting much booty in cattle. These
raids continued until the end of the war.[9]

The negotiations, discussions and debates that brought about
peace and ultimately the unification of South Africa made far
greater impact on the Protectorate than did the war.

The bogey of the Chartered Company was no sooner exorcised
than another arose. This was the possibility that the Protectorate might be transferred to South Africa. It made its appearance
during the discussions that prepared the Peace of Vereeniging,
when it was suggested that at least two of the three High
Commission Territories might be absorbed either by the Transvaal or by the Orange River Colony. However, the question was
closely linked with that of the non-European franchise regarding which there were divergent views. In order not to delay the
peace treaty the franchise issue, and by implication that of
transfer, were postponed until the introduction of self-government in the Transvaal and the Orange River Colony. But when
in 1906 and 1907 that happy event occurred, the two republics
showed clearly that they had no intention whatsoever of giving
the franchise to Africans. The question of transfer had once
more to be deferred, since the British Government refused to
hand over the territories without a reasonable assurance of an
African franchise.

The National Convention of delegates from the four self-
governing colonies of South Africa – the Cape, Natal, the
Transvaal and the Orange River Colony – sat between October
1908 and February 1909 to prepare a draft constitution fora
united South Africa. Lord Selborne, the British High Commissioner, warned the chairman, Sir Henry de Villiers, that the
transfer of the High Commission Territories could in no way be
assumed. 'The obligations of His Majesty's Government to the

tribes inhabiting Basutoland and the Bechuanaland Protectorate', he wrote, 'are obligations of the greatest possible weight.
These tribes surrendered themselves under the dominion of
Queen Victoria of their own free will, and they have been loyal
subjects . . . ever since. The history and connection of Swaziland
is different, but the obligations are different only in degree.' In
a later letter Selborne expressed himself even more strongly: 'It
is no question of policy that we are discussing; it is a question of
honour, and one in which every section of public opinion in the
United Kingdom, Government and Opposition alike, is keenly
sensitive.'[10]

The South Africa Act, which created the Union, was accepted
by the Imperial Parliament in August 1909 and came into
operation at the end of May 1910. Discussions in the Convention had done nothing to narrow the cleavage on the subject of
the franchise. Delegates from the Cape Colony favoured a form
of franchise for Africans; those from the north, that is from the
two Boer republics, were immovably opposed to any franchise
for Africans at all. This divergence and the known sensitiveness
of the British Government to matters affecting Africans, are
reflected in that part of the Act which deals with the transfer of
territories in South Africa 'belonging to or under the protection
of His Majesty'.

Section 151 provides that the King, with the advice of the
Privy Council, may transfer the government of these territories
to the Union on addresses from the Union Houses of Parliament. The territories would then be governed in accordance
with a special schedule to the Act, which embodied safeguards
for the indigenous people. There must be no alienation of land
in Basutoland or in the reserves of Bechuanaland and Swaziland; the sale of intoxicating liquors was prohibited; the custom
of holding tribal assemblies would continue. To secure observ-
ance of these safeguards there would be a special form of administration under the direct control of the Governor-General.

In the House of Commons Mr Asquith said that the Imperial

Government had 'a voice, and the ultimate voice' on the question of transfer. The Colonial Office spokesman more cautiously gave an undertaking that nothing would be done about transfer 'without the House of Commons being informed'. He added however that the wishes of the natives would be 'most carefully considered' before any transfer took place. Lord Crewe, speaking as Secretary of State for the Colonies, ominously gave utterance to prevailing opinion. 'It does not seem conceivable', he said, 'that for an indefinite future these areas should remain administered from here and that the new South African Union should have no lot or part in their administration.' Neither then nor later was it said that the transfer of the territories to the Union would be subject to the *consent* of the inhabitants.

It must be said that on the face of it transfer did not appear at the time to be an unreasonable proposition. The High Commission Territories are geographically and ethnically part of South Africa. The topography of Lesotho is perhaps a special case, but no outstanding landmarks separate Botswana and Swaziland from the rest of the sub-continent as, for instance, the Zambezi divides Rhodesia from Zambia. The Swazi are Nguni like the Zulu and speak practically the same language, while a man knowing only Tswana could travel from the Free State to Ngamiland through country inhabited by other Sotho and encounter no significant language barrier on the way. Economically, as we shall see, these territories are, or until now have been, largely dependent on South Africa.

The obstacles to transfer, and they were to prove fatal, were the opposition of the people most concerned and diplomatic stonewalling on the part of the British Government. The Tswana chiefs sent in petitions against transfer while negotiations for union were still proceeding, and this was only the beginning of a long campaign of resistance. From 1913 onwards, save for the period of the Great War, the issue was regularly raised by the South African Government and as regularly evaded or smothered by the British.

The British attitude towards the question underwent modification during these long exchanges. In 1909 there was no doubt in the mind of the Government that the destiny of the High Commission Territories lay with the Union, of which in the natural course of events they would some day form a part. Sooner or later, it was thought, the northern republics would come round to the more liberal outlook of the Cape on the political and social rights of Africans.

As time went on it became obvious that this was not going to happen. Northern intransigence remained quite unaffected by the influence of the Cape, and British opinion began to question the assumptions prevailing when the Act was drafted. The subjection of British territories to a racialist régime was now viewed with increasing repugnance. The British Government, though handicapped by the wording of the Act, which clearly contemplated eventual transfer, nevertheless stood firm on the original pledge that this would not take place until the inhabitants had been consulted and until Parliament had expressed its views. Moreover in 1923 the Duke of Devonshire gave an explicit assurance to a Swazi delegation that His Majesty's Government would not support any proposal for transfer if it involved the impairment of the safeguards in the schedule to the Act.

The South African Government became increasingly exasperated by the Fabian tactics of the British, and in 1934 General Hertzog, South African Prime Minister, declared that the position was fast becoming intolerable. But he brought nothing essentially new to the debate and he was told flatly that the time was not opportune to raise the question. 'All our information', said the Secretary of State for Dominion Affairs in reply, 'goes to show that the result of consultation with the inhabitants . . . would, at least so far as the natives are concerned, not be likely to be such as to enable transfer . . . to be proceeded with.' This belief was repeated more strongly in the following year.[11] At the same time a concession was made to the South African viewpoint in a proposal for co-operation between the

Union and the High Commission Territories in order to create among Africans a less distrustful view of transfer.

Meanwhile the constitutional background against which section 151 of the South Africa Act was conceived had entirely changed. The Statute of Westminster of 1931 and the Status of the Union Act of 1934 made it possible for the Union Parliament to alter the South Africa Act and its schedule in any way it wished. The safeguards so carefully devised in 1909 could be done away with, and neither the British Government nor the British Parliament would be able to do anything to prevent it. However, an assurance was given in a memorandum prepared by the Union Government in 1939 that the system of government that would be instituted on transfer would be that outlined in the schedule and that no departure from the terms of the schedule was contemplated.

Co-operation between the Union and the territories did not prove as fruitful as had been hoped. When the High Commissioner suggested that the Union might contribute £35,000 in 1936–7 towards a four- or five-year development programme, General Hertzog agreed at once, but the people of the territories were so reluctant to accept a gift from that source that the offer had to be withdrawn. A joint advisory council on co-operation, composed of the three Resident Commissioners and three Union officials, reported in 1939 but made no substantial recommendations. Indeed the report does little more than underline the economic dependence of the territories on the Union.

The Second World War, like the first, caused a lull in these exchanges, but they began again when peace came, especially after the Nationalists under Dr Malan came to power in South Africa in 1948. The new Prime Minister gave forceful expression to South African resentment at the implication that the Union was not to be trusted with the promotion or protection of African interests. But apart from 'grievous mistrust', said Dr Malan, there was another aspect of the question that South

Africans could not ignore. This affected the status of their country in the Commonwealth. South Africa, he went on, was compelled to harbour 'within her embrace, and even actually within her borders', territories that were 'entirely dependent on her economically, and largely also for their defence, but belonging to and governed by another country'. No other country in the Commonwealth, claimed Malan, would tolerate such a situation.

But the time had now almost vanished when the transfer of the territories to South Africa could even be thought of. The war had enormously accelerated the developing sense of responsibility towards colonial territories both in Great Britain and in the world at large. In this an important factor had been the contribution of African troops towards the Allied victory. The conduct of metropolitan Powers now came under the watchful eye of highly critical international organizations. Moreover in a world in which most people are coloured South Africa's racial policies seemed extremely offensive. The transfer issue became moribund in the 'fifties and received the *coup-de-grâce*, if it was not dead already, when South Africa became an independent republic in 1961.

XI · Political Changes

The war of 1914–18 afforded the Tswana an opportunity to serve overseas and a company from the southern chiefdoms went to France with the South African Labour Contingent. Otherwise the war made little impact on the Protectorate. An incursion by Germans from South-West Africa caused a mild stir on the western border and a band of Transvaal rebels entered the Protectorate from the east, but were quickly rounded up. An unhappy sequel to the war was the spread to the Protectorate of the influenza epidemic that swept the world in 1919.

In 1922 the Caprivi Strip, which had been part of German South-West Africa, was entrusted to the Protectorate Government to administer on behalf of South Africa, mandatory Power for the former German territory. This arrangement lasted until 1929 when the Strip was handed over to South-West Africa.

The decade following the war also saw the first systematic attempt to explore the Kgalagadi. In 1927 the European Advisory Council proposed that money should be provided to establish a cattle route across the desert. Accordingly, towards the end of the same year, Lieutenant Beeching of the Protectorate Police was ordered to make the route recommended by the Council. Starting from the west he crossed the desert in twenty-three trekking days with a scotch cart and oxen and five camels. As this was during the rains he had no difficulty about water.

Following this pioneering effort, an expedition under the Imperial Secretary, Captain the Honourable B. E. H. (later Sir Bede) Clifford, set out from Shoshong in 1928 to cross the desert westwards in motorized transport. In spite of great difficulties this journey too was successfully accomplished. Another expedition under Captain Clifford explored the area west of Nata in 1929, and in 1931 a route was surveyed for a railway from Bulawayo to Gobabis in South-West Africa through the Chobe Crown Lands and Ghanzi.

This was a period of important advances in Protectorate political life. The year 1919 saw the establishment of the Native Advisory Council, representing at first the southern chiefdoms. Khama held aloof and the Ngwato did not attend as full members until 1940. The function of this council was 'to discuss with the Resident Commissioner all matters affecting native interests which the members desired to bring forward'. Membership was composed of representatives from each tribe, of whom the ruling chief must be one. In principle the other representatives were nominated by the tribes 'in accordance with their custom', but in practice they were chosen by the chiefs. They were usually headmen, sometimes tribal officials, occasionally persons of standing like the late Dr S. M. Molema of Mafeking, medical man and historian, who represented the Rolong. In 1931 the Tawana joined the Council, in 1940 the sub-chiefs of the Francistown district sent representatives, two came from the Kgalagadi district in 1943 and one from the Chobe in 1950. In 1940 the name of the Council was changed to African Advisory Council, and in 1951 to African Council.

The meeting of the African Advisory Council, which took place once a year under the presidency of the Resident Commissioner, was an important and impressive event in the Protectorate calendar. There would be a formal opening, officials in full dress uniform, police guard of honour, assembly in a specially erected pavilion. The Resident Commissioner would deliver a 'speech from the throne', reviewing the past year and outlining plans and prospects for the future. He would then withdraw and leave the representatives to debate their agenda, with officials at hand to answer questions, make suggestions, produce papers, explain, if they could, the Administration's activities in any special direction, help frame proposals if that were necessary. Meanwhile the Resident Commissioner would talk to the representatives informally on any subject whatever, discuss affairs with district commissioners who had come from up-country for the occasion, and there would be a garden party at Protectorate House.

It was not perhaps the most democratic way of doing things. To the extent that the representatives were all either chiefs or chiefs' nominees the Council failed to provide 'popular' representation. But if one remembers that the chiefs were usually able men with a genuine sense of public duty, that Tswana society was essentially aristocratic, and that the discussions were always frank and sometimes heated, it will be appreciated that the Council afforded a real link between Administration and people. One has only to read the record of the proceedings to perceive the wide range of the debates and the ability of those who took part in them. It is true that the Resident Commissioner was not bound to accept the advice of the Council, but he would have been foolish to treat it lightly or ignore it.

The European Advisory Council was instituted in 1920 and held its first meeting in the following year. There were at that time about 1700 Europeans in the Protectorate, made up of residents in the farming blocks, traders in the reserves, and missionaries. The Council consisted at first of six members elected by Europeans in the six areas into which the Protectorate was divided for the purpose. This number rose to eight over the years. There were seven official members headed by the Deputy Resident Commissioner but these did not have a vote. The Resident Commissioner presided. The function of the Council was to advise the Resident Commissioner on matters affecting Europeans in the Protectorate, but as in the case of the African Advisory Council he was not bound to accept the Council's advice.

Khama, chief of the Ngwato, died in 1923 at a great age after a reign of nearly fifty years. He is buried at Serowe, capital of the Ngwato since 1902, and above his grave is the graceful figure of a duiker, totem of the tribe. On the plinth are the words, 'Righteousness exalteth a nation'.

Khama was succeeded by his son Sekgoma, then a man in his fifties. His reign was a short one and he died in 1925, leaving a son Seretse, who was still a little boy. Tshekedi, son of Khama's fourth wife Semane, was installed as regent during Seretse's minority. Tshekedi was then twenty years of age and was already showing those aspects of his character that made him, like his father, one of the best-known Africans of his time. He ran into trouble from the moment of his installation.

The first incident, involving the Rratshosa family, might well have cost him his life. Rratshosa was an important man among the Ngwato. Not only was he Khama's secretary and son-in-law but he was also of royal lineage, claiming descent from Molwa, the chief who immediately succeeded Ngwato, founder of the tribe. He had three sons, Simon, John and Obeditse, and Simon married Khama's grand-daughter Oratile. This family took Tshekedi's installation very badly and lost no opportunity to make trouble for the new regent. In April 1926, after a fierce quarrel, Obeditse and Simon fired on the regent in the *kgotla*. Tshekedi was only grazed, but two headmen, Gopolang and Kgosidintsi, were seriously wounded, though both recovered. For this crime Obeditse and Simon were sentenced to ten years' imprisonment (the sentences were reduced to four years on appeal) and several members of the family were banished. The case had an echo in civil claims and counter-claims which went as far as the Privy Council.

The Rratshosa troubles were probably the gravest to beset the young regent but they were by no means the only ones. The Rratshosa affair was followed by a dispute with the Khurutshe, comparatively recent immigrants in the Ngwato country, who wanted to set up a new Church in defiance of Khama's policy to have only one Church in his country, that of the London Missionary Society. Then in 1930 a man named Moanaphuti Segolodi, who had married into the family of Rraditladi, leader of the dissidents at Palapye in 1895, combined with other notables to bring charges of tyranny and oppression against Tshekedi. This ended with Moanaphuti's banishment.

Next came a claim to the chiefship by a man named Gasetshwarwe, son of Sekgoma the late chief by an irregular union. With his fellow-conspirator Kesebonye, Gasetshwarwe collected a number of supporters for his claim but was tried for sedition and sent to prison. On his release he went to live at Molepolole.

Dissensions also arose within Tshekedi's own household. In 1937 he repudiated the child born to his wife Bagakgametse, at the same time accusing the wife of attempting to poison him. In the subsequent divorce proceedings the name of Leetile, a grandson of Rraditladi, was freely mentioned. Subsequently Leetile and other descendants of Rraditladi went into exile.

Tshekedi had many fine qualities: determination, persistence, sincerity, eloquence, and a stock of good ideas on administration and development. But his life was too much taken up in quarrels with his people and with the Government, sometimes with both simultaneously. It seems unlikely, even by the law of averages, that these recurring squabbles were always wholly the fault of the other side. But Tshekedi was never one to concede that he could in any circumstances be wrong, and his combative instincts were fostered by the support he received from his well-meaning lawyer in Cape Town and from a number of people in England who looked upon this dynamic autocrat as their ideal of a liberal African ruler. A less talented man would have achieved more by occasional compromise and a willingness to admit that the opposition might sometimes have a point. Socially Tshekedi was gay, friendly, an excellent host and a stimulating travelling companion. The older members of the British Administration, who had as it were grown up with him, liked and respected him, though his differences with them were neither few nor small. Perhaps his greatest service to the Protectorate lay in his opposition during the middle 'thirties to the transfer of the High Commission Territories to South Africa. His campaign attracted sympathetic attention in Britain and provided a useful stimulus to public opinion.

The first of Tshekedi's many brushes with the Government was in connection with a mineral concession granted by Khama to the British South Africa Company. Tshekedi took exception to the concession and urged that it should be cancelled, declaring at the same time that both he and the Ngwato as a whole were opposed to mining in their country. The Government thought that an abrupt cancellation might lead to expensive litigation (legal opinion as to whether the concession could be cancelled was divided) and hoped that the tribe and the Company would negotiate a new concession. The negotiations were protracted and in 1930 involved a visit by the regent to England, where he had two less than cordial interviews with Lord Passfield, the Secretary of State. Nevertheless a new concession was signed in 1932. In order to smooth the course of negotiations the Government gave the Ngwato a substantial area of Crown Land in the north of their reserve, while the Company, in return for the new agreement and a satisfactory mining law, made over to the Government an area near the railway line occupied by the Tlokwa. This was the piece of land given by Setshele to the Tlokwa chief Gaborone as a home for the tribe (p. 70). Ceded by Sebele in 1895 as part of the railway strip, this land was formally transferred by the Government to the British South Africa Company in 1905, the Tlokwa staying on as tenants of the Company. Now on reverting to the Government the area was declared to be the Tlokwa reserve. In the event the Company abandoned their concession in 1934 but the Ngwato retained the Crown Lands which they had received from the Government, while the Tlokwa, beneficiaries of a transaction in which they had no direct interest, remained possessors of their own newly-acquired little country.

The next incident bordered on farce. In 1933 Tshekedi was accused of causing a European to be flogged in his *kgotla*. The facts are still not clear, and there is some ground for believing that the European in question, who was little more than a boy and had been interfering with Ngwato women, was not flogged at all but was struck by an incensed bystander. It was a matter that in almost any other dependency would have been quietly and quickly settled by a competent district commissioner, but it caused a commotion in South Africa, where opinion is acutely sensitive to anything that savours of humiliation of white by black. The Acting High Commissioner, Admiral Evans ('Evans of the Broke'), came to Serowe with a large escort of marines and the regent was solemnly deposed. Happily commonsense soon reasserted itself and he was reinstated shortly afterwards.

In the early 'thirties the British Government felt compelled to consider a change in the method of governing Africans in the Protectorate. There were several reasons for this. Generally, there was a more informed opinion in Britain in regard to colonies and a growing sense of responsibility towards them. No doubt the institution of the League of Nations and the allocation of colonial mandates to Great Britain contributed to this. Lord Lugard's great work *The Dual Mandate in British Tropical Africa* was another factor. Sir Donald Cameron's important innovations in Tanganyika attracted attention, and interest was further stimulated by various commissions that visited East and West Africa. The introduction of proper procedures for Colonial Service recruitment and for training probationers involved the universities, where the Colonial Administration began to replace the Indian Civil Service in esteem.

Less auspicious factors had focussed attention on African administration in the Bechuanaland Protectorate. In deciding an appeal that arose from the Rratshosa affair, the Privy Council expressly criticized the native custom that Tshekedi cited as his authority for burning the Rratshosas' houses. This custom, said Their Lordships, was 'incompatible with peace, order and good government', in the terms of Loch's proclamation of 10 June 1891.[1] At about the same time native custom also came under scrutiny in connection with the allegedly servile condition of the Sarwa (Tawana for Bushmen), and a commission of enquiry was appointed in 1931. Other matters that seemed to need investigation were the control of tribal funds, including the money occasionally raised by the chiefs for special purposes, and the 'regimental' system, which was really the use of the traditional age-grades to supply labour for public works, but sometimes for free service to the chief.

Ancient law and custom had served well enough in the past. But the repositories of tradition, the old chiefs and their councillors, had disappeared, to be replaced by young men educated, many of them, outside the Protectorate, and lacking the 'feel' of tribal administration. It seemed that the time had come in some degree to regulate and formalize the administrative and judicial systems.

The matter was exercising the Secretary of State at about the time the regent was in England in 1930. 'I had . . . intended', said Lord Passfield, '. . . to refer to the question of making statutory provision in order to establish on a proper legal footing the jurisdiction and powers of the Courts of the Chiefs in the Protectorate when trying cases in accordance with native law and custom.' Lord Passfield went on to say that the Resident Commissioner would be asked to frame proposals after consulting the chiefs and the Native Advisory Council, 'with a view to regularizing the position and giving the requisite legal sanctions to the Chiefs' Courts in the exercise of jurisdiction according to native law and custom'.

In 1931 the Resident Commissioner told the Native Advisory Council that the Secretary of State had instructed him to consider introducing reforms to the administrative and judicial systems, but he assured the Council that the chiefs and tribes would be fully consulted before any decisions were taken.

In 1933 two draft proclamations were put before the Council, having been discussed up and down the country since the previous year. Tshekedi, though still not willing to be a member, had been invited to attend the debates and he criticized the drafts as an encroachment on native law and custom. When they were enacted at the end of the following year, he challenged their validity in the Courts. In this he was supported by the young chief of the Ngwaketse, Bathoen II.

The two enactments were entitled respectively the Native Administration Proclamation and the Native Tribunals Proclamation, both of 1934. Their purpose was explained by the High Commissioner in a long, carefully worded memorandum that was issued at the time of their promulgation.[2] The object of the new legislation, he said, was not to abolish the existing method of administration, 'described nowadays by the term "indirect rule" ', but 'rather to provide for its continuance and its further development'. The two proclamations had been framed, he went on, 'with the intention of preserving the hereditary Chieftainship, preserving the exercise of tribal authority by the Chiefs, preserving native law and custom, and preserving the administration of justice by the native courts or Kgotlas, through making it possible for them to function satisfactorily under changed and changing conditions'.

This assurance did not satisfy the two plaintiffs. Although in the course of years the powers of tribal authorities had been eroded, the chiefs still held to the concept of parallel or dual rule. They believed that this had been promised to their predecessors by Chamberlain in 1895 and that the arrangements concluded then had the force of a treaty.

The chiefs' complaint against the proclamations was twofold. First, they said, the enactments changed certain native laws and customs, and this was a thing that the High Commissioner was not competent to do since the Order in Council of 9 May 1891 from which his power was derived bound him to respect native laws and customs. Secondly, they complained that the proclamations violated treaty rights enjoyed by the Ngwato and Ngwaketse chiefs and tribes.

The case came before the Special Court of the Protectorate and judgement was given by Mr Justice Watermeyer in the latter part of 1936. As to the chiefs' first point, the judge agreed that the new laws undoubtedly made important changes in native laws and customs. But, he said, the High Commissioner was not incompetent to make these changes. The word 'respect' in the Order in Council did not mean that the High Commissioner must be *bound* by native laws and customs, but only that he must treat them with consideration. This he had done by consulting the people and taking careful account of their objections.

As to the second point, the judge dealt with it by resorting to section 4 of the Foreign Jurisdiction Act 1890, which lays down the procedure for settling questions that may arise as to the existence and extent of the Crown's jurisdiction. In such a case, says the Act, it falls to 'a Secretary of State', on application by the court, to decide any such question and this decision is final. On being asked 'What is the nature and extent of His Majesty's jurisdiction within the Bechuanaland Protectorate?' the Secretary of State for Dominion Affairs replied that the Crown had 'unfettered and unlimited power to legislate for the government of and administration of justice among the native tribes in the Bechuanaland Protectorate, and this power is not limited by Treaty or Agreement'. This answer was conclusive and the chiefs' second point fell away. But even if the court had not resorted to this procedure the chiefs would have found it difficult if not impossible to show that any treaty of the sort they had in mind existed.[3]

So the chiefs lost their case and no one would suggest that the judge was unjust or the Administration unfair. Yet it is impossible not to feel with Lord Hailey some sympathy for the chiefs.[4] As a body the Tswana chiefs had shown themselves by no means obstinately hostile to change. In addition to Khama, many of whose measures sprang from a puritan morality, there had been some notably go-ahead tribal leaders. Such, for instance, were Seepapitso, chief of the Ngwaketse (1910–16), an outstanding man unhappily cut off before his early promise could reach fulfilment;* Isang, regent of the Kgatla (1921–9), regarded in his time as one of the most progressive chiefs in the country; and now Tshekedi himself.[5] Furthermore the Administration had hitherto shown no sign of wanting to systematize local government. The alterations brought about by the 1934 proclamations, necessary no doubt, perhaps even overdue, were too radical, too abrupt. 'There is a rhythm which must be observed in the development of a system of rule based on the use of traditional institutions.'[6] When, some years later, as we shall see, new legislation was passed to replace that of 1934, the atmosphere was much more harmonious and there was a much greater measure of agreement between the Government and the African Advisory Council.

* He was murdered by his brother because of some trifling grievance.

XII · The Economy and Social Services — World War II

The last chapter brought us to the eve of World War II, a convenient time to break off the general narrative and to look back on the economy of the Tswana as it developed to that stage in their history.

'The principal wealth of the [Tlhaping] country', said Henry Lichtenstein,

> consists in the breeding of cattle. Their herds are much more numerous than those of the Koossas [Xhosa], and they have as great a veneration for them. . . . Milk, whey, and cheese, are the favourite food of these people. The chase, besides, affords them a variety of food. . . . They pay much more attention to agriculture than the Caffres [Kaffirs]: their fields are commonly fenced round, and they cultivate, besides the Caffre-millet [sorghum], two sorts of beans, gourds, and water-melons. . . . The fruits of many sorts of trees that grow wild are also collected, and dried for winter stores.[1]

Substantially, agriculture and cattle-raising still remained the basis of the economy, the latter easily predominating. With the substitution of a money economy for exchange and barter (p. 74) a third element in the system assumed a growing importance. This was paid labour in South Africa.

The practice of migrant labour was no new thing to the Tswana; indeed Kwena are recorded as working on European farms as early as 1844. The discovery of diamonds in Griqualand West gave a strong impetus to the practice, and when Alexander Bailie was sent by the Griqualand West Administration on a recruiting tour in Bechuanaland, he had little difficulty in securing a promise from the chiefs to encourage the flow.[2] The discovery of gold on the Witwatersrand and later the expansion of South African industries served further to stimulate labour migration. At the end of 1933 the South African Government raised the ban on the recruitment of labour north of latitude 22° (it had been imposed because of the heavy mortality on the mines of men from those regions) and by 1940 there were 18,000 people from the Protectorate working for wages in South Africa at a time when the total population was believed to be about 300,000. When the 1971 census was taken, 46,000 Tswana, including 9000 women, were reported to be working outside the country, the great majority in South Africa. The reported figures are thought to be much too low, and the real number of absentees may be as high as 60,000–65,000. The social effects of this migration may be deduced from the report on that census, which says that 'on a national level a quarter of all males in the working age group were absent from Botswana at the time of the census and in the south east the level was much higher, rising from 30% in the Barolongs to 40% in the Ngwaketse, with the North East District in the same category with 32% absent'.[3] The rural economy must also suffer, since the tasks of agriculture and animal husbandry are left to the very old and the very young and to women, in other words to those least physically equipped to perform them.

The motives for going abroad for work are economic pressure owing to the lack of similar opportunities near home, and the social prestige attaching to a man who has experienced life in the outside world. Migrant labour is still an indispensable source of cash income for the Tswana and it has become as much part of their way of life as were initiation ceremonies and hunting in the past. With the growth of local industries, especially a mining industry, the flow of labour outwards may diminish, though not to any great extent in the foreseeable future. Meanwhile the economic needs of the Tswana can only be fully met by working for wages in South Africa, and until current developments in

Botswana reach a more advanced stage the practice will continue unabated.*

Botswana's domestic economy lies under the perpetual threat of an arid climate, with uncertain and badly distributed rainfall, a general scarcity of water and not infrequent droughts. The urban habit of the Tswana, as we have already seen,† has compelled them to adopt a system of lands and cattle posts which may be situated at a considerable distance from the towns. During and immediately after the rains, watering stock presents no difficulty. But when the pans and the pools dry up, the pressure on available supplies from a cattle population which is already too large becomes very heavy and the pasture in the neighbourhood of the few remaining watering points is damaged to the point of denudation. In seasons of exceptional water shortage, cattle become very poor, and if one bad season is followed by another, there may be heavy mortality.

In addition to the dangers of drought, cattle suffer from a variety of diseases, including foot and mouth, trypanosomiasis and anthrax. The most disastrous of these was the rinderpest catastrophe of 1896, which destroyed most of the Protectorate's cattle.

The cattle trade was, and indeed still is, almost entirely an export trade and the markets were formerly South Africa, the Rhodesias and the Congo. These were by no means assured markets and they were often wholly or partly closed through a number of causes. During the early part of the century exports to South Africa were stopped for years because of pleuro-pneumonia (lung-sickness) in the Protectorate. During the middle and late 'twenties a partial embargo was imposed on Protectorate cattle owing to the overstocking of the Johannesburg market. Foot and mouth disease has also periodically caused restrictions to be imposed on cattle exports, to the grave detriment of the economy.

* In this connection see pp. 170-3.
† p. 14 above.

Agriculture, like cattle raising, suffers from erratic rainfall, with the added disadvantage that the soil is inherently infertile. Traditional farming methods, so far from countering the disadvantages of the environment, operate only to aggravate them. Nevertheless satisfactory crops of sorghum, maize, groundnuts and pulses can be produced on the eastern side of the country, where conditions are more favourable. When the rains fail, as too often happens, considerable quantities of foodstuffs have to be imported. The steps taken by the Government and tribal authorities to improve agriculture and animal husbandry will be described in a later chapter.

For the first twenty-five years of its existence the Protectorate was chronically insolvent and there was an annual deficit that had to be made good by a grant-in-aid. From 1915–16, except for three years following the First World War, the budget was balanced, at times with something to spare. However, from 1928–9 until 1940–1 there was a deficit every year which was met at first from the accumulated surplus and when this ran out, by a grant as before. After 1941 no further grants were required until the special budgetary supplements that began in 1956–7 (see p. 152).

The Protectorate was established at a time when the Gladstonian budget was still a controlling factor in colonial policy. The grant-in-aid was conditional on strict Treasury supervision, and the zeal with which Their Lordships snatched pennies, especially in the early days, is hardly credible to the modern mind. In 1898, when approving an allowance of £70 a year to the police officer in Ngamiland for acting as magistrate in addition to his normal duties, they stipulated, as to the current year, that equivalent economies must be made under other heads of the Protectorate budget.[4] During 1906–7, when a reduction in the Resident Commissioner's entertainment allowance of £200 a year was in question, the Treasury proposed, as a consideration for maintaining it at the existing figure, that the cost of living bonus of subordinate officers should be abolished. Well might the Resident Commissioner say in his Annual Report for 1905–6, 'The Administration of the Protectorate is carried on with due regard to economy, and with consciousness of the fact that the deficiency has to be met by the Imperial Treasury.'

This climate was not favourable to the growth of social services and for long these were virtually non-existent. African education was for many years wholly in the hands of the missions, to whom the Government gave a small annual grant. A similar grant was made to Tiger Kloof, the new place of higher education established by the London Missionary Society near Vryburg in 1904 to replace the Moffat Institution at Kuruman. Protectorate Africans educated at Tiger Kloof have since given notable service to their country in the Church, in education and in the highest ranks of administration, as well as in trade and industry.

An interesting feature of the Protectorate scholastic system was the setting up from 1910 onwards of local committees representative of Government, missions and people, to control educational activities in each tribal area.

In 1919 the practice whereby some people of the Protectorate made a voluntary contribution to education was regularized by the establishment of the Native Fund. This represented the proceeds of a levy of three shillings, later raised to five shillings, on every adult male. The Native Fund, as its name implies, was to be spent on objects of benefit to the African people. Most of it was spent on African education.

Of public medical services there were almost none. In 1913–14 there was one whole-time medical officer, who was stationed at police headquarters at Gaborone, four part-time district surgeons who looked after government officials, and two hospital orderlies. There were no properly equipped hospitals. In a country in which cattle represented the principal economic activity, there was only one qualified veterinary officer in the whole Protectorate, and he was assisted by one stock inspector.

The revenue of the Protectorate was made up largely of hut tax, originally imposed in 1899 at a rate of ten shillings and in 1908 increased to twenty shillings; customs revenue, which by an agreement with South Africa was ·27622 per cent of the total import and excise duties of the Union; and various licences and dues.

The largest item of expenditure had always been the police. This was a wholly European force in the early days, and just before the divorce of the Protectorate from British Bechuanaland cost £89,000 in a budget of £148,000. Thereafter steps were very sensibly taken to Africanize the force, but in 1913–14 the Protectorate police alone still accounted for £35,000 in a budget of £67,000, as against £1800 for Veterinary, £740 for Medical and £1200 for Education. Twenty years later, with 34 Europeans and 232 Africans, the police cost £32,000 from a total expenditure of £187,000, which may be regarded as a more reasonable proportion.

Conditions improved during the 'twenties and early 'thirties, when social services were expanded on a modest scale. But they were still inadequate in 1933, the year in which Sir Alan Pim presented his report on the financial and economic position of the Protectorate.[5] Although Pim's mission was primarily financial, he also made far-reaching recommendations regarding the structure of administration.

Perhaps the most important effect of the Pim reports (he carried out similar missions in Basutoland and Swaziland) was to draw attention to the backward condition of the High Commission Territories. No one reading these reports could fail to make unfavourable comparisons with the position in other British African territories.

This is not the place to explore the disparities in detail. It may even be that Bechuanaland fared no worse than say Uganda or the West Coast colonies in *their* first years of British administration. But it does seem safe to say that the period of extreme stringency lasted longer in the Protectorate than in other British

African countries, and that steps to achieve adequate standards were taken later than elsewhere.

The reasons are not far to seek. The temporary and provisional nature of the Protectorate made it the worst possible prospect for the benevolence of the British taxpayer. Why waste good money on a country that was destined sooner or later to fall into the lap either of the Chartered Company or of the Cape Colony, or, later, of the Union?

As the bogies of Company, Colony and Union in turn receded, there was still another reason why the High Commission Territories lagged behind other dependencies. This had to do with the nature of the high direction in London. When the Dominions Office, marking the differentiation between the self-governing dominions and the dependent empire, was formed in 1924, the High Commission Territories were allocated to the new department, being regarded, as it were, as part of South Africa. The golden age of British colonialism passed them by. While governors like Hugh Clifford, Guggisberg and Cameron were giving new purpose to African administration under a Colonial Office vivified by the doctrines of Lugard, J. H. Oldham, Edwin Smith and others, the High Commission Territories were the responsibility of an inconsiderable section of the Dominions Office, itself by no means the most impressive of the great Departments of State. There were no doubt good reasons for this arrangement, particularly in connection with Anglo-South African relations, but it caused some loss to the Territories.

World War II made a much stronger impression on the people of the Protectorate than either the South African War or World War I. From the beginning of hostilities the Tswana chiefs offered their own services and those of their people, and the opportunity came when the war spread to the Middle East, where military labour was urgently needed. Elementary training was carried out at Lobatse and the first Tswana contingent of the Royal Pioneer Corps left for Syria in September 1941, to be followed by others in 1942 and 1943. The total recruitment of Tswana was 10,000 men, a striking achievement for a country with such a small population. Among the officers were several members of the Protectorate Administration, and the five regimental sergeant-majors were all either chiefs or closely related to the chiefs of their respective tribes.

Tswana troops served with credit in the Middle East and in Italy, and when V.E. day came there were Tswana on the borders of Austria and others close to Trieste among the Yugo-Slav partisans. They were no longer just labour companies. Some were trained as anti-aircraft gunners and others as smoke companies. The anti-aircraft units had a busy time during the Sicilian campaign and the smoke companies were also called on. At Salerno an anti-aircraft regiment with Tswana gun-crews took a prominent part; and when the allied forces were pressed back onto their beach-head, this regiment took on a field firing role and later advanced in this capacity through Italy. A party of fifteen Tswana visited England and took part in the Victory Parade in June 1946.

XIII · The Seretse Affair — Finance and Economics

Experience in applying the controversial proclamations of 1934 had shown that they needed considerable revision. A committee of the Native Advisory Council was appointed to consider changes in 1938, a task in which Tshekedi and Bathoen co-operated wholeheartedly. The matter did not come before the Council until May 1943, when the report of the committee was put before the members and was thoroughly debated. From these discussions there emerged later in the same year two new proclamations to replace those of 1934.

The harmony of the 1943 debates, in contrast to the heated nature of those that preceded the earlier legislation, was due to several causes. One was that the members had had experience of the tribal treasuries system established in 1938, and this had given them a new outlook on the possibilities that the system offered of financing local services. Secondly, the 1934 legislation had not in the event proved as vexatious as its opponents had expected. The third reason, and perhaps the most important, probably lay in the personality of the Resident Commissioner, Mr (later Sir Charles) Arden Clarke. This able official, recognizing that Tshekedi held the key to the successful outcome of the negotiations, handled the regent with great delicacy and tact. The new proclamations, while maintaining the ultimate authority of the High Commissioner, removed the features of the 1934 legislation which appeared to violate traditional laws and customs.

Soon after the war the Ngwato, who in the course of history had had their share of trouble with subordinate tribes, became seriously involved with the followers of Mswazi, headman of a group of Kalaka who lived in the northern part of the Ngwato reserve. The quarrel was of long standing. Mswazi's people had for many years shown their resentment of Ngwato rule by refusing to pay taxes, disobeying orders and sometimes by acts of violence. In 1947 Tshekedi resolved to have a show-down with the recalcitrants, and with the consent of the Administration sent in tax collectors supported by a tribal regiment to extract outstanding dues. The disconcerting result was that a large number of Mswazi's people fled across the border into Rhodesia, leaving their property behind them, and the Resident Commissioner then had the uncongenial task of negotiating for a home for the fugitives in Rhodesia.

The history of the Tswana in latter years sometimes reads like that of the Ngwato, and the history of the Ngwato is too often that of quarrels in the chiefly family. In the late 'forties began the most dramatic of the Khama dynasty feuds, one that not only deeply divided the tribe but also became a *cause célèbre* involving the British Government, and, because of the colour element, had racial and international repercussions. This was the Seretse Affair.

Seretse, it will be remembered, was the son of Sekgoma, Khama's son, and he was heir to the chiefship of the Ngwato. He was born in 1921, educated at Tiger Kloof and took his B.A. degree at Fort Hare College. In 1945, several years after he might have been expected to step into the chiefship, he was sent to Oxford and after a year at Balliol he proceeded to London, where he began to read for the Bar.

In September 1948 Tshekedi, busy at Moeng building a new secondary school, received a telegram from Seretse announcing his imminent marriage to an English woman, Miss Ruth Williams. To Tshekedi, a traditionalist fanatically jealous of the integrity of the tribe, this was a blow to the heart. That Seretse, heir to the chiefship, whom he had regarded as a son, should so flout the usages as to contract marriage without consulting the tribe was bad enough; but that the prospective bride should be, not a Tswana, not even an African, but a European, was to him intolerable. So the regent mobilized all his resources to dissuade Seretse from his impious intention. But the marriage took place later in the same month in spite of Tshekedi's efforts to stop it. Seretse then flew out to Serowe, and there were a number of tribal meetings in which the matter was discussed.

It is important to understand that never, at that time or later, was Seretse's right to the succession called into question, and allegations that Tshekedi challenged Seretse's conduct because he wanted the chiefship himself are not true. Nevertheless the tribe as a whole at first took the traditionalist view and resolved that Seretse's wife should be prevented from coming into their country.

Then the mood changed. In spite of Tshekedi's protestations to the contrary, the feeling grew that if the nephew should be prevented from taking his rightful place, the uncle would dig himself in for good. The tribe began to split, those supporting Seretse being considerably the larger section. It was said at the time that the family feuds of Khama's days were reflected in the manner in which the notables aligned themselves in the current dispute. However that may be, the third great meeting of the tribe in June 1949 produced a decisive majority for the installation of Seretse as chief with his European bride.

Upon this Tshekedi announced that he would leave the reserve, which he did, taking his supporters with him, including a number of influential men. He went to live just inside the Kwena country near the wells of Lephepe, where Seretse's father had spent part of his long exile during his estrangement from Khama. Tshekedi also asked for a judicial enquiry to advise whether Seretse should be recognized as chief, and if so, what would be the position of Ruth Khama and the children of the marriage.

A judicial enquiry into the question of recognizing Seretse was duly held. It was presided over by Sir Walter Harragin, Chief Justice of the High Commission Territories, and he was assisted by two senior administrators. This tribunal reported towards the end of 1949.

Exactly what the report contained remains a mystery to this day, for it was never published. The reason it was suppressed was that it contained matter that was uncongenial to the Government. However, the report did advise against the recognition of Seretse 'whose absence from the Bechuanaland Protectorate was essential to the peace and good order of the Bamangwato Reserve'.* Seretse was therefore invited to London so that he might express his views, and when these proved unacceptable it was resolved not to recognize him as chief. Meanwhile he would not be allowed to return to the Protectorate for at least five years and he was given an allowance to maintain himself and his family during his exile. At the same time Tshekedi was ordered to live outside the Ngwato country and forbidden to enter it without special permission.

So the position remained for three years or more. The District Commissioner was appointed Native Authority as a temporary expedient. Seretse was banned from the chiefship for ever by Order in Council, and the Ngwato drifted in political disarray without their natural leaders. Matters improved in 1953, when the admirable Rasebolai Kgamane stepped into the gap as Native Authority. He was the third senior member of the tribe after Seretse and Tshekedi, a war veteran and a quiet, solid man of integrity.

Meanwhile the position of the parties had changed dramatically in 1952 with the reconciliation of Seretse and Tshekedi and their resolve to confront the Government together. The government case, based largely though not wholly on the probability of ructions in the tribe, had until then been perfectly defensible. The danger was a real one and at the time certainly appeared to justify the decision to keep the two leading figures apart and

* 'Certain arguments are advanced and views expressed ... which are not accepted by His Majesty's Government, and with which they could not associate themselves' (Cmd. 7913).

out of the Ngwato country. But the risk of disturbances disappeared when uncle and nephew shook hands and it was then time for a generous gesture on the part of the Government. Tshekedi was allowed back into the reserve in 1952, when he went to live at Pilikwe, under the Tswapong hills. But the ban on Seretse was maintained until 1956, when he was permitted to return to his country as a private citizen.

It would have saved a great deal of trouble if the British Government had been braver, more honest. With hindsight it is now clear that Seretse should have been recognized as chief as soon as the danger of clashes between opposing parties subsided. No one doubted that the real reason why recognition was withheld was reluctance to upset South Africans, who on the subject of miscegenation are 'hardly sane'. As it happened, there were good grounds for not wanting to affront South Africa. If they had been stated or even hinted at they would have been understood.*

But Seretse was neither recognized nor was the true reason for withholding recognition admitted. This was partly because of the timidity of the Government in London, which was afraid to confess, even to its own backbenchers, that its attitude was

* The author may perhaps be permitted to interpolate a personal note. Early in 1950, when he was Resident Commissioner in the Protectorate, he spent a long afternoon trying to persuade the High Commissioner's Chief Secretary, Mr W. A. W. (later Sir Arthur) Clark, that the draft of Command Paper 7913 would not do, and that the situation required more candour, especially in regard to the South African factor. Everyone between Cape Town and the Zambezi had guessed the real reason for Seretse's exclusion and to hide it was merely to destroy the document's credibility. This plea was not accepted at the time, and the ambiguous wording of para. 17 of the Paper cannot be taken as a concession to the author's arguments.

There is little doubt that the decision not to publish the report of the Harragin enquiry was due to references in it to South Africa. A very senior Colonial Office official is said to have described the report as 'maladroit'. On the other hand, one of the two experienced administrators who sat with Harragin and who had known the Tswana for thirty years told the author that in his opinion publication of the report would have relieved the Administration of many local anxieties.

in any way influenced by reluctance to offend South African susceptibilities; and partly because of the fatal dichotomy in the office of High Commissioner which that prophetic Scotsman John Mackenzie had condemned, *mutatis mutandis*, seventy years earlier. Changes in the status and functions of the office had not removed the dangers that Mackenzie had foreseen. Sir Hercules Robinson's later successors were no longer governors of the Cape Colony, nor, as happened after Union, governors-general of South Africa. But they still governed three African territories and they were at the same time quasi-ambassadors to South Africa. They lived in South Africa, they shunted seasonally with the South African Government from Pretoria to Cape Town and back again, and they only emerged from South Africa for periodic visits to the territories. They were thus very much exposed to South African influences, and this must have coloured their advice to the Commonwealth Relations Office, itself not an organization of the calibre to take its own line and to resist the promptings of a strong High Commissioner. If we except Robinson's proceedings in 1884–5 (p. 67) there was no time when Mackenzie's warnings against the dual nature of the High Commissioner's office were more clearly vindicated than in the Seretse affair.

To the Protectorate Administration the affair was no picnic. Local officials naturally had their views on the matter. The older men, brought up in the Khama tradition, were perhaps inclined to be sympathetic towards Tshekedi. Younger ones, several of whom had sometimes been disturbed by Tshekedi's authoritarianism and had ventured to cross swords with him, may have thought that Seretse should be welcomed home without delay. But caught as they were between the upper and the nether millstones, they all knew that their first duty was to prevent rioting and bloodshed. And this except for one unhappy incident they did. Police detachments from Basutoland, Swaziland and Southern Rhodesia were welcome reinforcements, for the Protectorate police were hard pressed. Not so welcome was the cohort of journalists, some reasonable enough but others who might have come straight from *Scoop*.

On Seretse's return to the Protectorate in 1956 he became vice-chairman of the Ngwato tribal council, of which Rasebolai was chairman. Tshekedi was made secretary two years later. This gifted man died at the height of his powers in 1959. During the last years of his life he was particularly active in negotiating a mining concession with the Roan Selection Trust from which great benefits are expected.

Although the energies of the Administration were very much absorbed in the Seretse affair, a significant step forward was taken in the early 'fifties. The need for closer co-operation between the two advisory councils, African and European, had long been felt, and in 1951, after thorough discussion, a Joint Advisory Council was created. It comprised eight members from each council with four official members. It met twice a year under the presidency of the Resident Commissioner.

Meanwhile a silver lining had appeared in the economic clouds in the form of successive Acts providing for financial aid to British dependencies. Grants made to the Bechuanaland Protectorate under the first of these, the Colonial Development Act of 1929, were modest, and small loans were also provided for special works in 1932 and 1933. However receipts from the Colonial Development Fund increased steadily as the decade wore on, and in 1937–8 they had risen to nearly £70,000, which was more than a quarter of the Protectorate's total revenue. The Colonial Development and Welfare Act of 1940 and an amending Act of 1945 enabled a greatly increased scale of grants to be made and in a wider range. Between the years 1940 and 1950 expenditure rose from £40,000 to £105,000, and at the end of March 1951 the total amount received from Colonial Development and Welfare Funds since the Act of 1929 was £727,000. To this must be added commitments on schemes in progress amounting to £461,000 and a sum of £124,000 still uncommitted and available for expenditure up to 1956. Expenditure continued on an increasing scale during the 'fifties, reaching a peak of £452,000 in 1957–8. Between 1950 and 1960 £2,350,000 was spent from the Colonial Development and Welfare Funds on purposes that might be broadly grouped under the headings land use, mineral development, communications, education and health.

During the same period ordinary revenue more than doubled, from £554,000 to £1,200,000, and to this there was added yet a further bonus. Half-way through the decade the British Government, recognizing that it was impossible to maintain satisfactory standards of administration in so large and sparsely populated a territory until development had generated a larger revenue, decided to provide the Protectorate with a special grant-in-aid in order to maintain those standards 'at an approved minimum level'. This special grant began in 1956–7 and reached a figure of £650,000, or over half the ordinary revenue, in 1960. In the same period over £1 million was raised by way of loans. These were spent on public works and public utilities.

In 1959 an Economic Survey Mission was appointed 'to conduct a general survey of the requirements and natural resources of the High Commission Territories . . . and to make recommendations on the utilization of the financial resources that are or might be made available . . .'. The commissioners' report covered a wide field and the projects which they recommended would, they hoped, put the territories on the way to becoming 'viable economic units'. This aim they thought was a 'reasonable probability' in the case of Bechuanaland. The limiting factor here, says the report, is water, shortage of which hampers economic expansion at every turn. This had long been known, but the commissioners struck a new note in their insistence on the need for economy in the use of existing supplies, and on the principle that water should be paid for by all users.[2]

Increased revenue after the war led naturally to an expansion of several services. Details of the various undertakings may be

found in the Bechuanaland Annual Reports, but there is one
that calls for special mention here. This was the Bamangwato
College at Moeng, which sprang entirely from African initiative,
was paid for by money raised by Africans in addition to their
normal taxes, and was in a large measure planned by Africans.

The moving spirit was of course Tshekedi, who conceived the
college partly as representing his greatest service to the tribe,
partly in pious memory of his father. Moeng is a beautiful
secluded valley forty to fifty miles from Palapye and the reason
Tshekedi chose the place was because Khama loved it and had
an orange grove there.* Tshekedi threw all his formidable will-
power and drive into the project. A levy in cash or cattle
amounting to about £100,000 was raised by the tribe, labour
was supplied free by tribal 'regiments' and Tshekedi himself
was unwearyingly active, whether discussing matters with the
tribe, negotiating and not infrequently differing with contractors
and consultants, canvassing advisers official and unofficial,
planning buildings, devising a constitution, supervising labour
or dealing with the innumerable contingencies that occur in an
enterprise of this kind.

Apart from the controversies inseparable from any of
Tshekedi's undertakings there were some grievous setbacks and
hitches. Expenditure ran out of control and there was an
anxious time while the future was in doubt; the Seretse Affair
and its attendant troubles held up building operations. These
were not made easier by poor communications and the distance
of Moeng from the railway. Perhaps worst of all, the Moeng
valley was found to be unfavourable for building owing to the
presence of underground springs. Ominous cracks appeared in
the houses and costly remedial measures had to be taken.
However the work was completed at last, a witness to Tshekedi's
energy and devotion.†

* Conversation with author.

† Some say Tshekedi's ruthless determination to build Moeng cost him
a good deal of popularity during the Seretse Affair, when he most needed

Unhappily, pessimistic predictions voiced at the time but ignored by Tshekedi have since been justified. The concept of a specifically Ngwato college was found to be too narrow. In 1956 the constitution was revised and Moeng became a territorial institution, the Government assuming responsibility for all recurrent expenditure and for the cost of new buildings. The isolated position of the college has proved not only desperately inconvenient for the purpose of supply and administration but has also been a serious obstacle to the recruitment and retention of good staff. Moreover the concept of a remote boarding establishment is at variance with the present Government's educational policy. Although Moeng purports to offer a full matriculation course leading to university entrance, it is now by way of becoming an expensive liability.

---

public support. Others deny this. It is a difficult matter to prove either way.

XIV · Independence

For many African countries 1960 was the *annus mirabilis* in which they attained independence. Botswana too took an important step towards self-government in that year. In 1959 a committee of the Joint Advisory Council presented a report recommending that this council should be reconstituted as a legislative council.

The report was accepted and at the end of 1960 the Protectorate was endowed with a new constitution. This provided for an Executive Council of official and unofficial members; a Legislative Council consisting of official, elected and nominated members; and an African Council composed of official, nominated and elected members, and the chiefs or African authorities of the eight principal tribes. Election to the Legislative Council was on a basis of communal representation, with parity of numbers for Africans and Europeans. The functions of the African Council were to act as an electoral college for the African members of the Legislative Council, and to advise the Resident Commissioner on tribal affairs, African custom, and generally on matters affecting Africans in so far as they related to policy and administrative practice.

The new constitution probably did not come before its time. In 1960 events in South Africa caused a stream of refugees to cross the frontier into Bechuanaland. Between 1960 and 1964 more than 1400 refugees entered the Protectorate, some genuinely political, others merely dissatisfied with their economic and social condition in South Africa and seeking to avail themselves of political asylum. A number of the refugees were members of African militant organizations and they created a climate in which Tswana nationalism could develop. The emergence in 1960-1 of the first political parties in the Protectorate is not therefore surprising. They were the Bechuanaland Protectorate Federal Party and the Bechuanaland People's Party (BPP). Only the second need concern us here.

The founder and president was K. T. Motsete, a politician of the old school, a graduate of London University, a minister of the London Missionary Society and a schoolmaster before he turned to politics. The vice-president was P. G. Matante, a vigorous personality with a record of involvement in South African politics, where his sympathies lay with the Pan-African Congress. The party's secretary-general was Motsamai Mpho, a South African militant associated with the African National Congress and in politics to the left of Matante.

The BPP's programme included a demand for radical social and political reforms, the expulsion of white settlers, a new, Africanized constitution, the whole combined with the usual denunciations of racialism and British colonialism. The party appealed to the non-tribal population of the towns along the railway line like Lobatse and especially Francistown, and it was also supported by immigrants and refugees from South Africa. It was however plagued by internecine rivalry, and in 1962 Mpho was expelled for attempting to seize the leadership. Two years later Motsete was unseated by Matante who became president of the party in his stead.

Meanwhile another factor had entered into the situation. Concerned at the growing strength of the BPP, its radical nature and the threat which it held to public order and peaceful change, Seretse Khama, who was a member of both Legislative and Executive Councils, took a hand in the game. Early in 1962 he announced the formation of a new party, the Bechuanaland Democratic Party (BDP). This party naturally drew a great deal of its strength from the Ngwato, but it was and still is also the party of the countryside, of the farmers, cattle owners, herdsmen, the men of the tribes, who form the great majority of the people of the territory. In the towns the party appeals to the moderates, the professional and middle classes. The formation of the BDP, as we shall see, effectively dashed the hopes and ambitions of the BPP.

The emergence of political parties, organized on a national basis, made it possible for the Government to accelerate the tempo of political change. It was announced in 1962 that a constitutional review would take place in 1963. In spite of demonstrations organized by the BPP calling for the immediate abolition of the existing constitution, which was condemned as racial, the Government adhered to its timetable and constitutional talks began on 1 July 1963.

The results of the talks were announced in November 1963. The Protectorate would be given a form of self-government designed to lead naturally to independence. There would be a ministerial system, and the Prime Minister would be the member of the Legislative Assembly who commanded the support of the majority of the Assembly. The executive Government would be controlled by a Cabinet presided over by the Queen's Commissioner (about whom more below) and composed of the Prime Minister, the Deputy Prime Minister, up to five other Ministers drawn from the Legislative Assembly, and the Financial Secretary, who would be Minister of Finance *ex-officio*.

The Legislative Assembly would consist of a Speaker, thirty-two elected members more or less ('not substantially more nor substantially less') and four specially elected members. The Attorney-General and the Financial Secretary would also be members, the former without a vote, the latter with a vote so long as he remained a Minister *ex-officio*.

There would be a House of Chiefs, which would advise the Government on matters affecting Africans; and bills affecting a defined range of matters of concern to Africans must be referred to the House of Chiefs, and might not be proceeded with unless this was done.

During 1962 and 1963 Seretse's BDP was still getting into its

stride and the impetus for political change came from the protecting Power rather than from the activities of local political
parties. The constitutional proposals were approved by the
British Government with minor amendments in June 1964 and
registration of voters was carried out in the same year. The
number registered was 180,000, representing eighty per cent of
the potential electorate, and thirty-one constituencies were
delimited.

With the prospect of imminent self-government the BDP
grew during 1964 into a real political force. It was no doubt the
emergence of this party as an organized entity, with a programme and massive public support, that made possible the
rapid and harmonious political and constitutional changes of
the next two years. At the elections in March 1965 the BDP
swept the electoral board, taking twenty-eight of the thirty-one
seats, the remaining three going to Matante's BPP. Seretse
Khama was asked to form a government and thus became Prime
Minister of the country's first African government.

Coincident with these constitutional advances and forming
part of them was a change in the Resident Commissioner's title
and status. At the end of 1963 he became Queen's Commissioner, an office that carried the status of Governor, responsible
to the Colonial Office instead of as heretofore to the Commonwealth Relations Office through the High Commissioner in
South Africa. Under the new constitution the Queen's Commissioner retained control of external affairs, defence and
security. In 1964 the office of High Commissioner itself was
abolished.

Both these changes were long overdue. 'The High Commissioner', said *The Times*, 'seems an unnecessary link in the chain,
and it might be advisable to let the Resident Chief [sic] Commissioner at Mafeking deal direct with the Colonial Office.' The
issue was that of 16 June 1896.

A further change took place about this time, a small but not
insignificant one. With the introduction of self-government

the term 'Protectorate' was no longer appropriate, and the territory became plain 'Bechuanaland'.

From the grant of self-government in 1965 events moved swiftly. The election manifesto of the BDP had declared that the party favoured independence as soon as possible. The new Government accordingly lost no time in asking Great Britain to declare a date for this next step. In October 1965 the British Government replied that independence would be granted on 30 September 1966, providing that all were ready. A constitutional conference was held in London in February 1966 (from which Matante withdrew in a huff when his protests and demands were ignored), a constitution was hammered out, and the Republic of Botswana came into being punctually on the date that had been forecast. There could be only one choice for Head of State, and Seretse Khama, who was knighted in the same year, duly became President of the Republic.

The approach of self-government had thrown into sharp relief the anomaly of a headquarters not only outside the Protectorate but also, since the secession of South Africa from the Commonwealth in 1961, in a foreign country. This was not a new question, for the idea of a move had been canvassed several times in the past, though never seriously pursued. In the early 'sixties the matter became urgent, and the decision was taken to build a new capital at Gaberones, now Gaborone, on the railway a hundred miles north of Mafeking. Originally Mosaweng, this was the place that was renamed after Gaborone, chief of the Tlokwa, who died there at the reputed age of 106 in 1932.*

There were many sound administrative and economic reasons for moving the capital into the Protectorate and the psychological ones were no less cogent.† As was correctly said, the creation of a new capital would provide a tangible symbol of national sentiment and would bear witness to the primacy of

---

* As to how the area occupied by Gaborone's people became the Tlokwa Reserve, see p. 131.
† *Annual Report* 1964.

national interests. The removal was effected smoothly in spite of the difficulties of the task, and the first phase took place according to schedule in February 1965.

The building of a new capital at Gaborone was only one part of a 1963–8 economic plan for spending twelve million pounds on development. The plan was designed to expand the social services, encourage private enterprise and local initiative, improve agriculture and the livestock industry, assist mineral production and foster tourism.

With the constitutional developments of 1965 a new phase of economic development opened for Bechuanaland. The victory of the BDP, the prospect of a stable government and the announcement of a realistic economic policy with a pledge of continued co-operation with neighbouring trading partners created a good climate for investment. Secondly, as the Annual Report delicately put it, 'The introduction of internal self-government and the elections made it possible for popularly-supported economic policies and objectives to be developed and adopted.' (This means that an African government can get away with unpopular measures more easily than can a European one.) Taking a long view, the outlook on the economic front was promising.

But meanwhile the economy was immediately threatened with disaster by the drought, which by 1965 had persisted unbroken for four and in some places for five years. It had cost the country 400,000 head of cattle, or almost one third of the national herd. Cattle in marketable condition were sold for slaughter. Over 100,000 people were on famine relief, the loss of crops was almost complete, reserves of food and money were practically exhausted and there was a considerable move of people to the towns.

Counter-measures of course were taken. The Prime Minister launched a National Relief Fund; large mining houses in South Africa increased the quotas normally applied to mine labour from Bechuanaland; and help was obtained (after some delay owing to a dock strike in the United States) from the United Nations World Food Programme. As a remedy for the long-term effects of the drought, plans were laid for an important programme of rural rehabilitation.

In concluding a chapter describing the end of British rule in the country now named Botswana, one may be excused for quoting the President's own words at the independence ceremonies. 'It would be wrong of me', he said, 'not at the outset to state again, as I have done so frequently before, the great gratitude of my people for the protection and assistance which have been given to Botswana by the United Kingdom during the long period of our dependence. . . . Though we are very proud that we ourselves are now independent, and politically free to make our own way in the world, it should not therefore be thought that past affections and regard have been immediately erased. We look forward to a continuing association of pleasant friendliness in which the ties of the past may in some sense be preserved.'

XV · Modern Times

ECONOMICS AND SOCIAL SERVICES

Gaborone, custom-built capital of Botswana, is a town of 18,000 inhabitants, situated on the railway from Cape Town to Rhodesia in the old 'Gaberones Block'. It lies partly on the Government 'camp' of Protectorate days, and partly on farms acquired from former freehold owners. The town is imaginatively planned in a shape somewhat resembling an ellipse flat on one side, with ring roads on the periphery and an inner system of roads and walkways, the latter farsightedly reserved for pedestrians.

Gaborone has most of the amenities of a modern town. Shops (providentially sited in a car-free shopping precinct), hotels, a cinema, a public library, a broadcasting station, a museum, a stadium, several fine churches and elegant government buildings, of which the most striking is appropriately the House of Assembly. The Botswana wing of the University of Botswana, Lesotho and Swaziland, at present in makeshift buildings, will soon be housed in a new campus of its own.

Private houses in Gaborone are attractive in appearance and many of them are surrounded by pretty gardens, which testify, in this harsh climate, to much patient effort on the part of the owners. The roads have been planted with trees, though there are not yet enough of them, and ornamental shrubs are growing on the roundabouts and in some of the public places.

Fortunately there is now enough water for all purposes. This is provided by a dam on the Notwane river three miles from the town, which has created a lake seven miles long. The lake is not only a public utility; it is also a valuable amenity.

Gaborone is still growing, and houses, offices and new roads are being built in all quarters. There is a serious shortage of low cost housing which the local authorities are making strenuous efforts to meet, but many Africans attracted to the capital by the new affluence live under conditions that must cause anxiety. There is some unemployment since there are now more people here than there are jobs for them. In fact Gaborone already has an 'urban problem', still in its early stages but serious enough to create concern.

Fifty miles south of Gaborone, also on the railway, situated in a range of hills, lies Lobatse, site of one of the largest meat processing plants in Africa. Lobatse also has several smaller industries but a shortage of water has prevented the town from growing as fast as Gaborone. Now a pipeline is being built from the Gaborone dam, which, it is thought, holds enough water not only for the capital but also to supplement the deficiency in the Lobatse supply.

Francistown in the Tati area is the traditional industrial centre of the north and may assume even greater importance with the advent of large-scale mining at Selebi-Pikwe and Orapa.

In contrast to these bustling modern towns life in the rural areas goes peacefully on, basically in the same way as it has always done. The great tribal centres have hardly altered through the years, and the hub remains the home of the chief and the *kgotla* or meeting place. The seasons still dominate the most important activities, and the people spend their lives as in the past between the town, the lands and the cattle post. Ploughing, sowing, the harvest and the care of their cattle are their principal occupations, and their chief concern is the incidence of rain.

Foreign Aid

There can be few independent African countries that have so engaged benevolent international attention as Botswana. This has resulted in a remarkable flow of grants and loans for a variety of purposes as well as a considerable influx of expatriate manpower.

This was due to a variety of reasons. Clearly the discovery of copper, nickel and diamonds was one, but the surge of interest that has attracted assistance from many different sources has its origins in something more diffuse. The attractive personalities of the President and Lady Khama and their romantic history was certainly one factor, the modesty and tact of the new Government another. The poverty of the environment as a whole offered a challenge to the organizations concerned with under-developed countries, while the Okavango and Chobe region excited the interest of naturalists and conservationists. Some nations are in part moved by the belief that to help Botswana is to discomfit South Africa, whose designs are by definition evil. Last but not least, the cheerful goodwill of the people, their maturity and their commonsense, make Botswana a very pleasant place to work in.

Projects supported by foreign aid cover almost every field of economic and social activity and are too numerous to describe in detail. A sample list, representing only a fraction of the total number, is given in the table on page 166. The estimated revenue for development in 1972–3, most of it from foreign sources, was £22½ million, and the largest item, excluding mining development at Selebi-Pikwe, was a loan of £2 million from the United Kingdom.

The foreign community of Botswana, which is itself a form of foreign aid, is diverse and cosmopolitan. It includes diplomats, civil servants, resident or visiting experts, businessmen, academics, teachers and social workers. There are a large number of volunteers, some good, some not so good, on whom the education system greatly depends. And there are teams of foreign workers who are here to carry out schemes to which their respective countries are committed. Many of these expatriates are consciously working themselves out of a job. For instance the civil servants will disappear as soon as enough

Tswana qualify to replace them. Similarly no doubt the university will in time be largely staffed by Tswana or at any rate Africans. Fewer volunteers will be needed in the schools as more local-trained teachers come forward. Foreign worker teams will presumably go home when their particular scheme is completed. One hopes too to see the emergence of a class of Tswana entrepreneurs and businessmen. Meanwhile the foreign community plays an essential part in the life of the country and it is difficult to see how, without them, present standards could have been so rapidly attained.

Substantial foreign aid has not deterred the Tswana themselves from seeking their own economic salvation. One of the basic objects of the 1970–5 Development Plan is to achieve financial independence so that recurrent expenditure shall be covered by revenue generated within the country. This object has already been attained. The new Customs Agreement negotiated with South Africa, Lesotho and Swaziland brings in greatly increased customs revenue and enables Botswana to dispense with the large United Kingdom grant that has supported the budget since before independence. Mining revenue will also contribute substantially to budgetary stability, while other revenue items to show an increase are income tax and income from tourism. Excluding some comparatively small sums from Great Britain specifically earmarked for pensions and certain other emoluments, the estimates of recurrent revenue and expenditure for 1972–3 balance at about £12¾ million.

Para-statal Corporations

On the theory that some operations are more economically and efficiently carried out by independent agencies than by the direct action of the Government, there have been set up a number of para-statal organizations to take over the functions of government in certain technical, financial and commercial fields. The oldest of these is the Botswana Meat Commission, whose essential role in the cattle industry will be described later.

Examples of Foreign Development Aid (from the *Estimates of Revenue and Expenditure for the Development Fund, 1972–3*)

		Source
Expansion of Botswana Agricultural College	£109,700	UK
Grain storage	3,800	UK–FFHC
Dryland farming research	5,700	ODA
Livestock industry development	358,700	SIDA, IDA
Underground water development	12,400	UK
Small dam construction	7,800	OXFAM
Elephant and buffalo research	4,400	South African Wild Life Fund
Small enterprises promotion company	60,500	SIDA
Development of computer facilities	59,600	UK
Central training unit	166,600	DANIDA
Maternal and child health clinics	27,300	UNFPA, UNICEF
Four health centres	19,800	UK
Mahalapye Hospital	77,800	UK
Tutume Secondary School	41,500	McConnel Foundation
UBLS	257,000	UK
Automatic telephone exchanges	101,600	Standard Bank[1]
Expansion of broadcasting services	101,200	UK
Botswana–Zambia Road	540,500	USAID

ABBREVIATIONS TO TABLE:

DANIDA	*Danish International Development Agency*
FFHC	*Freedom from Hunger Campaign*
IDA	*International Development Association*
ODA	*Overseas Development Administration (UK)*
SIDA	*Swedish International Development Agency*
UBLS	*University of Botswana, Lesotho and Swaziland*
UNFPA	*United Nations Fund for Population Activities*
UNICEF	*United Nations International Children's Emergency Fund*
USAID	*US Agency for International Development*

[1] Though not strictly 'foreign', this item is included to show the variety of sources from whence aid comes.

The Botswana Power Corporation and the Water Utilities Corporation have responsibility for the supply of power and water to Lobatse and Gaborone. Later, probably in 1973, they will take over the corresponding facilities of the Shashe complex at Selebi-Pikwe. The activities of these corporations will in due course spread across the territory, and a long-term objective is rural electricity supply.

The National Development Bank gives credit facilities, mainly in small amounts, to commercial undertakings and farmers – a favourite is borehole undertakings – and the Botswana Housing Corporation builds housing for the public and private sectors for sale or renting. This corporation also stimulates house building generally. The BHC only functions at present in Gaborone, Lobatse, Francistown and Maun but it will extend its operations to other places as time goes on, including Selebi-Pikwe in 1973 or 1974.

The Botswana Development Corporation, unlike the others, which are established by statute, is a registered company in which the Government has 100 per cent of the shares. The BDC acts as a holding company for most of the shareholdings of the Botswana Government, and it also looks for and identifies other investment opportunities. This corporation has established several offshoots, notably a company associated with developments at Selebi-Pikwe.

All these organizations are independent in the sense that Government does not interfere with the detail of their work. At the same time they operate within a broad framework of rules and principles and each is answerable to the Minister responsible for the sector into which the activities of that corporation fall. The Minister appoints the Board but this does not imply that the majority of members would necessarily be official. These corporations are expected to pay their way (this includes servicing their loans) and even to make a modest profit. It was financial failure that caused the now defunct Botswana Airways Corporation to come to grief. There is fortunately no

sign that those corporations at present in existence are likely to
follow this precedent.

The Land

However much the economy may become diversified, the land,
on which eighty per cent of the population now depend for a
living, will remain for many years the most important source of
domestic income and employment.

Agricultural production rises little above subsistence level
and the principal crops are sorghum, maize, millet and cowpeas.
As in the past agriculture is concentrated on the eastern side of
the country, which is the area of better rainfall. But the rains
are as erratic as ever and the years between 1961 and 1966 were
a period of drought, the most serious drought occurring in
1965–6.

Meanwhile the evils associated with African husbandry show
no sign of diminution. Indeed the picture is even more depressing than before. H. A. Fosbrooke, in a survey of an area which
he regards as typical, refers to severe degradation of the soil,
environmental deterioration and declining productivity. 'The
rural situation in Shoshong', says Fosbrooke, 'as indeed in
many parts of Botswana, is well and truly in reverse, and indeed
. . . the rate of backward motion is in fact accelerating.' To
describe in detail all the causes of the present situation would
require a volume in itself. Broadly speaking they may be sum-
med up in the phrase 'inefficient land use', and they are probably common to many African countries where similar or near-
similar conditions exist. Fortunately the evil is not irremediable
and much can be done, the spirit willing, to recapture and con-
serve the vanished fertility. 'The land . . .', he adds, 'responds
readily to treatment and the present trend of deterioration can
be reversed by the implementation of sound management
measures.' He goes on to list a number of measures whereby, he
believes, the backward motion may be stopped and the vehicle
put into forward gear.[1]

The cattle population of Botswana or, as it is called, the national herd, amounts to over $1\frac{1}{2}$ million head. The drought of 1965–6 killed a great many, causing a reduction of 30 per cent in numbers, but the herd seems since to have made a good recovery. We have already seen the importance of cattle in Tswana life and it is unlikely that this will be sensibly diminished by modern developments. Indeed the contrary may well be the case, for whereas in the days when Lichtenstein visited the Tlhaping cattle were conserved as a sign of wealth and position, the practice of selling stock for cash has slowly grown and in Shoshong, for instance, accounts for 55·6 per cent of all the income of all the households in the village.[2] The same is probably true of most of the rest of Botswana. Nevertheless the traditional prestige attaching to the ownership of cattle persists and many farmers are still reluctant to part with their stock for slaughter. The annual off-take from the national herd remains low, being only about 8 per cent a year. It is surely not too much to expect that in time this proportion will increase and that cattle will assume a growing importance to the Tswana not only as a symbol of wealth but as wealth itself, convertible by sale into cash for the purchase of the other necessities of life.

All Botswana's beef exports go through the abattoir and cold storage at Lobatse, founded by the Colonial Development Corporation in Protectorate days and now managed by the Botswana Meat Commission, a statutory corporation formed in 1966. The abattoir can handle over 1000 head of cattle a day and the main export is chilled carcases, though boneless beef is also an important product. The abattoir sells not only beef but also by-products such as hides and skins, bone and blood meal. The market is overwhelmingly an external one, as it has always been, but the direction has changed. The principal consumer is now Great Britain, followed by South Africa and Zambia. Efforts are being made to open new markets and a somewhat unexpected customer is distant Hong Kong. The growth in

Botswana of mining towns like Selebi-Pikwe will no doubt create a modest internal market.

That the Government is aware of the need to improve Tswana husbandry is clear from the prominence given to the subject in official pronouncements. The two objectives of the Government, which are complementary one to another, are to prevent the land from deteriorating still further and to improve the condition of rural communities so as to reduce the influx to the towns.

There are at present three rural training centres, one at Sebele near Gaborone, where there is quite a complex of institutions concerned with agronomy, one at Mahalapye, and one at Maun in Ngamiland. At these centres demonstrators are trained for work in the field and intensive courses are given to selected groups of farmers. Other means of instruction are a mobile film unit, agricultural shows, decentralized group instruction and a farm broadcast from Radio Botswana. More rural training centres are planned. It is clearly not intended that farmers should suffer from lack of advice and guidance.

But what if education should not keep pace with exploitation and persuasion fail? The Agricultural Resources Conservation Bill, which was before the Assembly in October 1972, gives the Government power to enforce the adoption of proper practices when blandishments prove unsuccessful. Local conservation committees will be established in the districts to keep watch, and to stimulate public interest in conservation. At the centre an Agricultural Resources Board will receive the recommendations of the committees and will make rules and orders both individual and general. A great responsibility will thus rest on the local committees. The country will be fortunate indeed if it can produce enough men with sufficient persistence and courage to implement policies that are sure at first to be unpopular.

Minerals

It will be remembered that before Tshekedi Khama died he negotiated a mineral concession with the Roan Selection Trust

(see p. 151). The outcome of this concession was the discovery
of copper-nickel occurrences in the Selebi-Pikwe area some
sixty-five miles south-east of Francistown. Proven and probable
ore reserves at Selebi and Pikwe in October 1969 were stated to
be 45·7 million short tons.

Before these great deposits can be exploited there must first
be created a broad base from which to work. This base, in-
elegantly called the infrastructure, consists of a completely new
township which will include all proper services, power and
water facilities, roads and railways, posts and telephones,
government offices, schools, a hospital, a police station and a
gaol. Finance for this immense undertaking, which is estimated
to cost £32 million, is provided largely by loans from CIDA,
IBRD, IDA and USAID* as well as by smaller specific grants
from the United Kingdom and elsewhere. The mines themselves
are operated by Bamangwato Concessions Ltd, a subsidiary of
Botswana RST, and work has begun in the Pikwe mine.

The two most sensational aspects of the infrastructure are
undoubtedly the Shashe Dam and the power station. The dam
is being built on the Shashe river fifty miles north-west of
Selebi-Pikwe and water will be brought to the new township by
pipeline underground. The dam is just under eighty feet high
and two miles long, and the area of the reservoir is about 4200
acres. It is said that the supply will be sufficient for all industrial
and domestic purposes, including, happily, the watering of
gardens, a boon in this arid countryside.

The first thing that one sees on approaching Selebi-Pikwe
from the air or from the ground is the chimney of the power
station, five hundred feet high, a landmark for many miles. The
chimney has alas already claimed a victim, for one of the steeple-
jacks engaged in its construction fell from it to his death almost
on the day when it was completed. The furnaces still had the

* Canadian International Development Agency; International Bank
of Reconstruction and Development. For IDA and USAID, see abbreviations to table, p. 166.

appearance of great steel skeletons at the end of 1972 but the smelter was complete and the whole construction is due to be finished towards the end of 1973. Fuel for the power station will come by rail from the new colliery at Morupule near Palapye. Railways are being laid to connect Morupule and Selebi-Pikwe to the main line at Palapye and Serule respectively.

In the township work of a less spectacular kind is proceeding fast. There are already a number of permanent houses; roads are under construction; and all other preparations are being made to meet the needs of urban man. Meanwhile banks, businesses, shops, schools and government offices operate on temporary sites which will be abandoned when the time comes for them to move to their proper places on the township plan. One day this new town, built literally and figuratively on copper and nickel, will have a population of 25,000.

The other important mineral development of recent years has been the discovery by De Beers of diamonds at Orapa, about a hundred and forty miles west of Francistown in the northern Kgalagadi. As at Selebi-Pikwe, a completely new town has been built and production of diamonds has begun. It is known that the pipe contains a high proportion of industrial diamonds compared with gemstones.

Beside these two giants other mineral developments look modest but they are still significant. In addition to the copper-nickel deposits at Selebi-Pikwe, Bamangwato Concessions Ltd have found copper at Matsitama, about fifty miles west of Francistown. A subsidiary of the same company is investigating the possibility of producing common salt, soda ash and sodium sulphate from the brine deposits of the Makgadikgadi. In addition to Morupule there is another large coalfield at Mmamabula, which is on the railway eighty miles south of Palapye. There are known to be other more or less important mineral deposits in several parts of the country.

The most immediate benefit from mining is obviously an

increase in revenue. It is estimated that by 1975 Orapa and Selebi-Pikwe between them will produce a direct revenue of £7–8 million. This will do no more at first than ensure budgetary stability, but as revenue increases money will be released for development. There will also of course be a considerable indirect return which does not need to be analysed in detail here.

One thing, however, is not to be expected, and that is that the new mines will absorb any large proportion of the labour that now flows to South Africa. In fact it is not expected that the Selebi-Pikwe and Orapa mines will provide employment for more than 3000 workers, of whom 390 at first will be aliens. Another 2000 may find employment in associated activities. These are not large figures compared to the 46,000 Tswana who were at work in South Africa in 1971. However, Botswana is an expanding field, and the number of local labourers employed within the country will increase with the growth of mining and with the development of industries generated by mining.

Water

The most important mineral of all is water and the lack of it is still the greatest obstacle to the development of the territory. Since the early days of the Protectorate several thousands of boreholes have been drilled to provide water for human beings and for stock. Boreholes assisted by extraction from sand rivers have made possible the development of most of Botswana's towns. But the towns have outgrown their supplies and they suffer acute seasonal shortages. Similarly in the country the old complaint is as valid as ever. Natural water points for both stock and humans are few and far between and they are by no means always reliable. Crowding of stock around them means overgrazing and overtrampling of the grass and is thus one of the chief causes of erosion.

This is not to say that potential water resources do not exist. The Okavango Delta is itself a huge reservoir, at present hardly exploited. Its problems and possibilities are being investigated.

Of more immediate economic significance is the watershed of the Limpopo where over 80 per cent of the population of Botswana live, and where a very large volume of water runs to waste every year. This area offers opportunities for the building of dams and weirs which would greatly reduce this annual loss.

The use of water is regulated by the Water Act of 1967 and a Department of Water Affairs was created in 1969. A Ministry of Mineral Resources and Water Affairs will be established in 1973.

Communications

The road system remains basically the same as it has been since the country first came under European administration. A main highway, successor to the old 'missionaries' road' into central Africa, runs up the eastern side of the country parallel to the railway. From it there are branches going east and west to the important towns. The terrors of the old Francistown–Maun route across the northern Kgalagadi have been exorcised and it can now be travelled by car in reasonable comfort. There is a road from Kanye to Ghanzi across the Kgalagadi. It is marked secondary on the map, but this is not a journey to be lightly undertaken. A new road is at present being built from Francistown to Kazungula. In conjunction with a ferry across the Zambezi this will give direct road access to Zambia. Secondary roads and tracks connect the railway to some of the larger villages and the whole country is criss-crossed with sandy tracks more or less passable to wheeled vehicles.

The most convenient form of transport in a country like this is air transport. But experience in Botswana has shown the economic difficulty of running an airline when there is really not enough traffic to support it. Attempts to run scheduled services external and internal were not financially successful and were discontinued. Aviation in Botswana is now in the hands of Air Botswana Ltd, a subsidiary of the Botswana Development Corporation, itself the commercial arm of the Botswana

Government. This company performs no flying operations itself, but sub-contracts them to other companies. On this basis Protea Airways of Johannesburg runs a regular service on the route Johannesburg–Selebi-Pikwe–Francistown–Maun, and small aircraft operations, mainly charter, are sub-contracted to Esquire Botswana Airways. Besides controlling these activities on the part of its sub-contractors, Air Botswana is general sales agent in Botswana for South African Airways, BOAC and Zambia Airways. It also performs ground handling functions for incoming airlines at Gaborone and Francistown.

There are over fifty landing grounds in Botswana. Gaborone Airfield is used by South African Airways for scheduled flights to Johannesburg and as a stage in flights between Johannesburg and towns further north.

When all is said and done, the most important element in the Botswana communications system is still the railway, built by Cecil Rhodes in the eighteen-nineties. This has always played a central part in the country's economy not only as the main vehicle for imports and exports but also as the carrier for the overwhelming proportion of internal tonnages. The railway represents as it were the spine of the country on which all other forms of transport hinge. It belongs to and is operated by Rhodesia and is of course the only rail connection between Rhodesia and Cape Town.

Tourism

Tourism may be said to have taken Botswana by surprise. Ten years ago the territory was unknown to the tourist, although it possessed the basic requirements. Now, as in several other parts of Africa, especially East Africa, tourism is one of the faster-growing industries.

Botswana has much to offer the visitor. There are great herds of game, not so ubiquitous as in the past but still surviving in almost undiminished numbers in the north and north-west. There is excellent fishing in the Okavango and Chobe rivers.

Bird life is immensely plentiful and varied, while for the sociologist, the antiquarian and the historian there are African towns, planned and managed in the traditional ways, Zimbabwe-type ruins, Bushman rock paintings and sites evocative of the early European missionaries and explorers.

The Government has been quick not only to grasp the revenue-earning potential of the country's fauna, but also to appreciate the importance of protecting wildlife in order to maintain a sound ecological balance. There is a devoted and competent Department of Wild Life and National Parks. Nearly 30,000 square miles have been set aside as conservation areas, including the Chobe National Park of 4300 square miles. The Chobe Park is believed to provide a wider spectrum of wild animals than any sanctuary in the world.

There is one aspect of the tourist industry that has no flavour of the out-of-doors. This is represented by a gambling casino at Gaborone. Swaziland and Lesotho have similar casinos, and all three attract large numbers of visitors from South Africa, where this kind of indulgence is frowned upon. The effect of these establishments on local society has been the subject of anxious speculation, and there are some who think that the revenue, which is undeniably high, may be dearly bought. However, visitors may also make excursions to rock paintings, the ruins of Livingstone's house at Kolobeng, a vultury at Otse and two proposed game parks.

To those of us who think that it is no longer decent to decorate the person or the home with the remains of wild animals, the display at the local crafts shops in Gaborone is painful. Gazelle skins as mats and chair covers, *passe encore*, since we know that the former occupants were killed by hungry men for food. But the genets mummified in that fine kaross played a beneficent role in the ecology and deserved a better reward than to be hunted down and sewn together as a mat.[3] Exhibited no doubt to attract thoughtless visitors, wares of this kind serve to sustain a trade that many people would be glad to see die, and conservationists must hope that the Tswana will turn instead to a craft of a less destructive nature.

Education

However dilatory emergent nations may be, for instance in building drains or in improving the nutritional standards of their people, mention education, says Stephen Hearst, and 'a messianic exultation grips the countenances of ministers, an exultation that knows no equivalent in modern Western society'.[4] It may be that Western society, after the experience of many centuries, has come increasingly to question the purpose of education, its methods and especially its results. No such doubts assail the emergent countries. In Botswana, since independence education has received the highest priority and the achievements at least in the secondary sector have been impressive. Rapid expansion has been possible through the employment of expatriates, nearly half of them volunteers, who in 1970 constituted 85 per cent of the total number of teachers employed in the secondary schools. The results in the primary schools have been less dramatic. Many primary schools are severely handicapped by overcrowding and all suffer from a lack of well-qualified teachers. There is however a programme for improving primary school facilities and considerable emphasis is placed on teacher training. As qualified teachers come forward they will improve the quality of teaching in the primary schools and replace the expatriates who now support secondary education. There is unfortunately a considerable wastage of young trained teachers who find employment in commerce and the civil service.

The Maru a Pula (rain clouds) secondary school on the outskirts of Gaborone is a private fee-paying boarding school for all races and both sexes. It was founded and is run by a former headmaster of a well-known school in South Africa, a dedicated educationalist who combines boundless energy with idealism. In mid-1973 the buildings were not yet finished and there were still only fifty-five pupils in the school (they include two sons of Botswana's President). However more are expected in the coming academic year, and Maru a Pula should develop into a fine secondary school of an unusual kind. The spirit is that of Gordonstoun: self-reliance and service to the community.

St Joseph's School, Khale, near Gaborone, an old Roman Catholic foundation, is generally regarded as the most efficient school in the country at present. But a comparative newcomer, Moeding College at Otse, is surely historically the most interesting. Moeding is the Tswana name, 'at the spring', of the place called Tiger Kloof where the London Missionary Society established its well-known institution (p. 73). Tiger Kloof did not fit in with the policies of modern South African governments (it was a 'black spot' in a white area) and the missionaries had to leave in 1955. After continuing under government control for some years until a new (government) school was built at Mafeking, the institution was abandoned and the buildings now stand empty and neglected, a sad sight for passengers on the railway from Bulawayo to Cape Town. In 1963 the London Missionary Society resuscitated Tiger Kloof at Moeding, and by all accounts the new institution promises to be fully worthy of the old.

An interesting feature of education in Botswana is the 'Youth Brigades'. These are groups of young people who learn crafts and skills while working under an instructor on some particular undertaking. Carpentry, bricklaying, farming, weaving, tanning, mechanics and textile manufacture are taught under this system, and the work produced by the pupils covers most of the running costs of their training.

For older students the Botswana Training Centre in Gaborone provides vocational training in technological and commercial subjects, as well as courses for administrators and professional men. Higher education is represented by the Botswana wing of the University of Botswana, Lesotho and Swaziland. Here students may read for the first part of their degree before proceeding to complete it usually in Lesotho but in some cases elsewhere. The visitor from the West notes with misgiving that undergraduates still show a bias towards the arts degree, and is only partly reassured by a recent improvement in science teaching in the schools, and by the higher status which it is proposed to give to agriculture in the school curriculum.[5]

The Government is alive to the need to gear the education of the young to the conditions in the world in which they will live. At the same time there is a tendency to overstate the role of education as a means of supplying the country's trained manpower. That educated men are needed no one doubts. But there must be a limit to the number of graduates, especially arts graduates, of other than top quality, that a country like this can employ at a salary that graduates will expect. The prosperous West is reaching that point already after less than a generation of serious university expansion. Perhaps the answer is for more emphasis to be laid on education simply as an all-important element in a rich, full life rather than as a way to a job. It is a difficult, perhaps an impossible thesis to get across, but at least it will not arouse expectations that may be disappointed.

Health

Botswana with its cold winters and dry climate is regarded as a generally healthy country, although there is malaria in the north and north-west and sleeping sickness in Ngamiland. Malaria occurs in southern Botswana at times of heavy rain and there is bilharzia on the eastern side of the country, also in small pockets in Ngamiland. Apart from these, the common diseases of Botswana are enteritis, venereal disease, tuberculosis and pneumonia. During periods of drought there is malnutrition and scurvy, especially among children. The rate of infant mortality is still relatively high.

The ratio of doctors to population in 1970 was one to 24,000 persons, and there was one registered nurse to 2592 people. There is also a staff of health inspectors.

The larger towns have hospitals, including mission hospitals, and the smaller areas are served by health centres. And, to make the picture complete, there is one flying doctor, a Seventh Day Adventist missionary, who flies out from Kanye to visit places in the Kgalagadi. Voluntary bodies, for instance the Red Cross, play a valuable part in the public health system of the country.

Planning for the Future

The National Development Plan for 1970–5, in the words of the Vice-President, is a rolling plan. This means that it is constantly under revision and review, and a new plan document is published every two or three years, showing the results that have been achieved to date.

The Plan is for the most part dependent on finance from international sources and from foreign governments, but development revenue also includes grants from a number of voluntary agencies like, for instance, OXFAM. Something over half the money was in sight when the Plan was drafted, while the rest remained to be raised. No one seems to doubt that this balance will be forthcoming.

The Plan governs almost every aspect of national life, ranging alphabetically from agriculture to wild life conservation. The budget is naturally dominated by the Shashe complex, that is the development of the Selebi-Pikwe mines and all that goes with them. This is by far the largest item. Next come Public Works, Agriculture and Veterinary, Water Development, Education and Medical.

The total projected capital expenditure from 1970–1 to 1974–5 was originally £54 million. This included £19 million for the Shashe complex, for which the estimate is now very much higher.

A plan is only a statement of intention and itself constitutes no guarantee that it will be realized. It is only as good as the people who have to carry it out. The best plan will fail if the will to implement it is weak and faltering, or if it fails to enlist the co-operation of the people whom it is designed to benefit.

One may assume that provided the geologists have made no mistake and provided, further, the price of minerals is maintained, mining in the hands of large companies will do all that is expected of it. But the difficulties in other fields were underlined by the President himself in the foreword to the Plan. 'The greatest challenge ahead of us', he said, 'is undoubtedly that of rural development. The transformation of rural communities everywhere presents an intractable problem. . . . Rural change inevitably comes slowly and involves great efforts on the part of the people themselves.' At the same time the Vice-President enunciated the principle with which no one will quarrel, that the emphasis is to be on *persuasion* rather than *compulsion*. This presupposes an enormous fund of patience and perseverance on the part of instructors and other workers on the ground, as well as an adaptability to new methods among the farmers that is not often found in this kind of rural community. Much will depend on the personality of the men upon whom in the first instance implementation of the Plan will devolve. Owing to localization of the public service expatriates are increasingly giving way to Tswana officials. To these the President has already addressed a warning. 'I have told the civil servants', he said, 'that I would judge our localization programme to be successful "when we have not only replaced expatriates with local officers, but when these local officers are carrying out their duties as energetically and competently as their predecessors, if not more so".'[6] In all those parts of the Plan in which the willing, active co-operation of the people is essential, success or failure will depend on the dedication and pertinacity of the civil servants.[7]

POLITICS LOCAL AND NATIONAL

To anyone who knew Botswana in the years before independence, the most striking change and perhaps the most unexpected is a revolution in the system of local government. Until the last decade local government was entirely associated with the chiefship, and the chiefs were both tribal and national leaders. Despite the restraints imposed on the chiefs' powers from time to time, they remained the media through which the Protectorate was governed. No important administrative step could possibly be taken without their advice and consent, while in local matters the jurisdiction of the chiefs assisted by their councils was virtually complete. No other form of constitutional advance was envisaged but one primarily based on and evolved from traditional forms of government.*

The process although a slow one had worked reasonably well. The Tswana ruling families have in the course of history thrown up remarkable men, who combined vision and strength of character with considerable powers of leadership. It may be conceded that dynastic rivalries have sometimes caused temporary disruption in the life of the tribe, though perhaps not worse than the troubles caused by political and religious feuds in other communities. It must also be admitted that some chiefs were excessively autocratic, but the charge is by no means general. Most chiefs exercised their functions in the usual democratic African way. Once the respective powers and responsibilities of the tribal authorities and the British administration had been sorted out, the Protectorate enjoyed local government that was considered at the time to be both decent and effective, and of a kind that most people understood.

However in 1964 the Legislative Assembly decided that the growing complexity of administration and the expanding needs of a settled community demanded the reform and reorganization

* For the powers of the chiefs in the past, see pp. 12–13.

of local government. 'It became apparent that Botswana's rapid
constitutional advance at the centre should be matched by an
efficient and democratic system of local government.'[8] It was
decided to set up councils elected on a basis of universal adult
suffrage. The country was divided into nine district council
areas and three town council areas (Gaborone, Lobatse and
Francistown). Following local council elections, the new councils came into being on 1 July 1966.

The councils handle a large recurrent revenue derived from
rates and local tax, school fees and various other fees and dues.
They spend most of their money on education, which is by far
the largest item, followed by health, housing, works and
general development.

The councils have also prepared plans for long-term capital
expenditure, mainly on primary education, water resources and
health. These plans have called into existence a complicated
mechanism of village development committees, council planning committees and district development committees, all of
them in some way concerned with the preparation, co-ordina-
tion or implementation of the plan. As if these were not enough,
local conservation committees supervise the use of agricultural
resources in the districts and stimulate public interest in conservation; while in addition to the committees there are also
land boards which have taken over the chiefs' functions as
distributors and allocators of tribal land. Somewhere in the
middle of the maze lurks the figure of the District Commissioner.
This official was expected in Protectorate days to do most of the
work and if things went wrong to take all the blame. Perhaps he
still is.

We have come a long way from the old system, under which
the chief and his councillors ran tribal affairs with the minimum
of paraphernalia little more than ten years ago. District
councils, development committees, conservation committees
and land boards have taken over all the powers of the chiefs
other than their judicial powers (they still preside over the

customary courts), and even these have been curtailed by law. Moreover the tribal administrations have no assets of their own, and are entirely maintained by subventions.

The Government has no doubt that the policy is right. 'In each area of the country there is a democratically elected body with important local government functions and a vested interest in local development, able to contribute towards the general progress of the country by its ability to mobilize self-help in its various forms and to administer local projects of economic and social betterment.' [9]

Basic to policy towards the chiefship, both at the centre and in the districts, is the urge to replace the concept of tribe by that of nation. It is an aim shared with all modern independent African governments, who regard tribalism as divisive. The non-Tswana elements in the population, always strong numerically, are more influential now than in the past, and the desire to weld the population into a homogeneous whole without other distracting loyalties is comprehensible. But it is possible to be less optimistic than the Government as to the effect of the new order on the rural economy. One might, for instance, ask whether local elected councils, which do not command the respect previously accorded to tribal office holders, will be able to enforce an effective system of land use control. On the face of it this may seem unlikely, but it is pertinent to mention that the chiefs, who have lost their power but not their influence, may also be members of the local councils. Most Tswana still hold the chiefship in reverence, and the rural voters, when presented with several council candidates, tend to favour representatives of the aristocracy. Thus the new organs of local government may acquire something of the lustre of the old. It is also fair to say that in several places, after a hesitant start, local councils are working quite well. [10]

The central Government in Botswana, unlike the indigenous governments of several other countries, is remarkably close to the simple farming communities that make up most of the population. This is not only because the Government owes its existence to the mass vote of a predominantly rural electorate. It is also due to the great personal interest that many leading personalities, including the President himself, take in agriculture and cattle raising. Most prominent men have a stake in farming and are thus very conscious of the difficulties that face ordinary people. After all, they face the same difficulties themselves!

Another pleasing feature of modern Botswana is the dignified simplicity of the Establishment. This is no clique of *Wabenzi*,* pompous parvenus anxious to express their importance in extravagant display. Tswana society avoids this kind of vulgarity. Here the style of life is comparatively frugal yet comfortable, informal and relaxed yet courtly and civilized. In Gaborone one may often in the evening meet a Minister walking home from his office and exchange a word with him. One may see his wife shopping in the Mall or pushing a pram along Independence Avenue. Ministers' houses may have one or two rooms more than those of other mortals but they are no more ornate or ostentatious. A senior official's car may well be, like that of his British predecessor, a light truck or jeep suitable for getting out to a remote village on rough earth tracks. Salaries are moderate and as far as one can see there is no official corruption.

Under the Constitution of 1966 the Government of Botswana consists of the President, the Vice-President, the Cabinet, a Parliament consisting of the President and the National Assembly, and a House of Chiefs. The President holds office during the lifetime of one Parliament, normally five years, and whenever Parliament is dissolved there must follow a presidential election. The effect is to link the office of President closely to the Assembly and in theory it is possible for there to be a

---

* A term applied in East Africa to arrogant 'high-ups' who are privileged to ride about in Mercedes-Benz cars.

new President every five years, or less if Parliament is dissolved earlier.

A presidential election is a complicated and ingenious business which begins on a countrywide basis and later narrows to a majority choice by the elected members of the Assembly. Any citizen of Botswana of thirty years or more who is qualified to be elected to the Assembly may be nominated as a presidential candidate provided he can muster the support of a thousand voters. If only one candidate is nominated, he is declared to be President. But if more than one presidential candidate is nominated then every *parliamentary candidate* must declare which of the several presidential candidates he supports. If he fails to do this, his own nomination as parliamentary candidate becomes void. Finally, when the parliamentary elections are over, the presidential candidate who is supported by not less than half the elected members of the Assembly is declared to be President. By an Act of 1972 the President is now an *ex-officio* member of the Assembly and is not obliged to represent a constituency. The system of pre-selection of their President by parliamentary nominees might run into the difficulty, at present wholly theoretical, that in an Assembly with an even number of elected members, as it is now, support could be equally divided between two presidential candidates. But there exist parliamentary procedures to get over this difficulty.

The Vice-President is appointed by the President from any of the members of the National Assembly. The Cabinet, which advises the President on policy and on matters referred to it by the President, is composed of the President himself, the Vice-President and the Ministers.

The National Assembly has a total of thirty-eight members of whom thirty-two are now elected while the specially elected members still number four. In addition the Attorney-General is a member *ex-officio*, as also is the Speaker if not already an elected member. The Attorney-General has no vote.

The present Assembly is overwhelmingly composed of

Seretse's BDP although the majority is smaller than it was in 1965. The Opposition now consists of seven members, drawn from three different parties. At the 1969 elections the BPP retained their three seats; the BIP (Botswana Independence Party) gained one; and a new party, the Botswana National Front, won three seats, all in the Ngwaketse area. The leader of the BNF is the former chief Bathoen II, who in 1969 relinquished the chiefship to join the Opposition, taking the vote of his tribe with him. His personal prestige, deep ancestral roots, sincerity, experience and rejection of political claptrap make him the most weighty figure on the opposition benches.

Small as it is the Opposition is a welcome feature of the political scene though cynics might say that if it were to grow so large as to be dangerous it would soon be abolished. Even more welcome is a growing spirit of criticism among backbench members of the ruling party. There is no revolt against policy upon which all are generally agreed. But there is an increasing readiness to query administrative methods and procedure, and this, coming from the Government's own supporters, can do much to curb 'the insolence of office'.

There are pessimists who predict that the Botswana Democratic Party may lose more seats at the next election and the emergence of large urban populations in places like Gaborone and Selebi-Pikwe certainly make this possible. Such agglomerations always provide waters in which left-wing politicians may fish with profit. But no one suggests that the loss will be great or that the position of the ruling party will be seriously shaken.

The House of Chiefs occupies but a shadowy place in the Government of Botswana and it has only limited powers. The House can do little more than delay legislation affecting tribal affairs and the chiefship itself. The chiefs tend to interpret their terms of reference fairly widely and sometimes extend their discussions beyond the confines of the tribe to matters of territorial interest. At a recent meeting, for instance (11 October 1972), the Order Paper included a question on the control of bush fires and a motion on the deterioration in the behaviour of the country's youth. That the chiefs are worried about the decline in their status is shown by a motion on the same paper in which they asked the Government for an assurance of the position of their House 'in its role of administration'.

In addition to the four executive and legislative organs described above, the Constitution also established a judicature composed of a High Court with unlimited original jurisdiction in civil and criminal proceedings and 'such other jurisdiction and powers as may be conferred on it by this Constitution or any other law'. The judges are the Chief Justice, at present (at the end of 1972) a Nigerian, who is appointed by the President, and such number of puisne judges as may be prescribed by Parliament. The puisne judges are also appointed by the President acting on the advice of a Judicial Service Commission. The High Court normally sits at Lobatse, where the Chief Justice has his residence. The judicial hierarchy is completed by the Court of Appeal consisting of a president, a number of judges of appeal (at present from South Africa), and the Chief Justice and judges of the High Court. The Chief Justice may be president of the Court of Appeal if Parliament so provides. A further appeal may in certain cases lie from the Botswana Court of Appeal to the Judicial Committee of the Privy Council.

Finally the Constitution sets up two commissions, one the Judicial Service Commission which appoints and controls the Registrar of the High Court and the magistracy, and also appoints the Delimitation Commission which periodically reviews the constituency boundaries. The second is the Public Service Commission which considers disciplinary appeals from the public service and is responsible for public service examinations. Recruitment and appointments to the public service, always excepting those appointments specifically designated in the Constitution, are the responsibility of a Directorate of Personnel.

The Botswana Constitution has so far survived virtually un-changed, and this is a tribute to the men who devised it in 1966. No one in the Government evinces any wish to alter it except occasionally in matters of detail, and there is no one outside the Government who has any prospect of altering it by force. Mean-while the democratic procedures which the Constitution provides seem to be working well and to the contentment of all. There is no reason to expect any sensational changes in the near future.

In all emergent countries everything depends on the person-ality of the national leader, and Botswana is no exception. The position of Sir Seretse Khama appears at present impregnable, and it is well that this should be so, for there is nobody in sight who is capable of taking his place. The President combines the charisma that among the Tswana attaches to a member of a great chiefly family with the traditional aristocratic virtues of geniality and accessibility. Less generous personalities might have remained embittered by the difficulties which as a young married man he was called upon to face. But neither Sir Seretse nor Lady Khama appear to bear resentment for the past. Content to let bygones be bygones, they take the world as it is now.

It is a world of which the President has a realistic apprecia-tion. He has a clear view of his country's needs but entertains no illusions as to the ways of meeting them. If there is one theme on which he insists more than another it is the abolition of rural poverty and the development of a prosperous agriculture. This, he hopes, will be a counter to the worst effects of rapid in-dustrialization: a large influx of peasants to the towns and the growth of a shiftless urban proletariat.

In his foreign policy the President steers a middle course between the two extremes of nationalism – African and Afrikaner. As a good African he must reject South Africa's racial policies and he does so in language that is firm and uncom-promising and refreshingly free from clichés and cant. But he is fully aware of Botswana's economic and strategic vulnerability, and his utterances on international matters are studiously moderate. He is especially careful to avoid any appearance of wishing to interfere in the affairs of other countries.

Botswana's most immediate foreign preoccupation is naturally with South Africa and on this question the Government's attitude is well reflected in a paragraph in the *National Development Plan 1970–75*. After recognizing Botswana's dependence on South Africa the passage continues: 'It is considered to be in the interest of both countries to transform this dependence into a relationship of inter-dependence. Despite the differences in political and social systems, and the disparity of wealth and resources between the two countries, and given the close economic links, Botswana and South Africa have achieved, and wish to maintain, a stable relationship based on inter-dependence, co-existence and mutual non-interference.'[11]

The President's cautious statesmanship secures for Botswana the advantages of living without friction alongside a rich and well equipped neighbour, at the same time retaining the goodwill of other African leaders who from less exposed positions are able to reject all concessions to any aspect of the South African system.

XVI · Conclusion

That, briefly told, is the history of Botswana from the time when Europeans first came to southern Bechuanaland to the present era of independent nationhood. Several themes go to its making. First the spirit of evangelism that sent men of the calibre of Moffat, Livingstone and Mackenzie to proselytize the Tswana and then to become their teachers, advisers and in time defenders and advocates. More than to any other agency it is to the mission at Kuruman that the attachment of Bechuanaland to Great Britain was due, and the Tswana were fortunate in that early in their relationship with Europeans they had such disinterested and devoted sponsors.

Next is the geographical position of the country as the main road from the Cape Colony into central Africa. British missionaries and traders were the first to use it, but the Boers whom the Great Trek had brought up to the borders of Bechuanaland cast their eyes upon it, seeing in British influence along the road a barrier to their own expansion to the west and to the north. Later Bechuanaland became Rhodes's springboard for the colonization of Mashonaland. In 1884–5 the importance of the road in southern African and international politics, merging with humanitarian and economic considerations, impelled the British Government to make of Bechuanaland a British protectorate.

A third important element in Tswana history is the character of the Tswana themselves. Patient and enduring, these people have a singular talent for survival. They have produced remarkable leaders: Montshiwa, Sekgoma I of the Ngwato, Setshele, Khama, Lentswe, to name only the more famous, were brave, shrewd men. These qualities, and the loyalty that the people bore towards their chiefs, helped the Tswana to come through the vicissitudes of the nineteenth century, although, like the battle of Waterloo, it was 'a damned nice thing – the nearest run thing you ever saw in your life'.* Without British intervention it could hardly have been done.

Bechuanaland was a British protectorate for over eighty years, a period which it is now fashionable to describe as one of neglect. It is indeed true that 'development' came late, but there are other aspects of administration that are sometimes forgotten by the critics and yet are basically more important than the promotion of material well-being. These are the human aspects, the relations between government and governed. In spite of the controversies that so often occurred during Tshekedi's regency, and finally the matter of Seretse Khama's marriage, there are few British dependencies where those relations were easier and goodwill more lasting than in Bechuanaland. This reflects as much credit on the Government as on the people and should surely be counted against a deficiency in the public services. In any case these were by no means neglected in the last twenty or thirty years of British rule.

The last theme in Tswana history is the reaction after World War II of colonial peoples against European government, together with a sharpened attitude in the world at large towards the principle of colonialism. During the two decades after the war the 'wind of change' brought independence to most of Africa. It blew harshly in some countries, for example the Congo and Algeria, where it caused waves of devastation. Over Bechuanaland the wind was mild and the British Government withdrew in 1966 in a climate of good will.

The Tswana as usual found the man for the occasion. A member of a family that has played an outstanding part in their history now presides over a young nation that holds its future in its own hands.

* Wellington to Creevey.

Notes

CHAPTER I

1. John Barrow, *A Voyage to Cochin-China*, pp. 388–9.
2. Ibid., p. 390.
3. There seem to be hearsay references to them as far back as 1661 (C. C. Saunders, 'Early knowledge of the Sotho', in the *Quarterly Bulletin* of the South African Library, No. 3, March 1966). Captain Robert Gordon probably met some Tlhaping near the Orange river in 1779 but did not reach any of their large settlements.
4. Barrow, *A Voyage to Cochin-China*, p. 395.
5. Henry Lichtenstein, *Travels in Southern Africa*, vol. II, p. 393.
6. W. J. Burchell, *Travels in the Interior of Southern Africa*, vol. II, p. 389.
7. Lichtenstein, *Travels*, vol. II, p. 377.
8. Burchell, *Travels*, vol. II, pp. 366–7.
9. Ibid., p. 366.
10. Lichtenstein, *Travels*, vol. II, p. 412.
11. Burchell, *Travels*, vol. II, p. 182.
12. D. T. Cole, *Introduction to Tswana Grammar*, pp. xv–xx.
13. G. B. Silberbauer, *Report on the Bushman Survey*.
14. *Report on the Population Census 1971*. Precise figures are as follows: Tswana (including 45,735 absent from the country) 619,518; aliens 10,861. The Tswana figure includes the 10,550 nomads. The report suggests (p. 69) that there is an under-enumeration of 3 to 4 per cent, perhaps more.
15. Isaac Schapera, *A Handbook of Tswana Law and Custom*, p. 19.
16. Burchell, *Travels*, vol. II, p. 313.
17. Lichtenstein, *Travels*, vol. II, pp. 413–14.
18. Schapera, *Handbook*, pp. 62–72.

CHAPTER II

1. John Campbell, *Travels in South Africa*, p. 245.
2. Ibid., p. viii.
3. Moffat, *Missionary Labours and Scenes in Southern Africa*, pp. 228 et seq.

4. Barrow, *A Voyage to Cochin-China*, p. 387.
5. *Missionary Correspondence*, pp. 18, 53.
6. *Apprenticeship at Kuruman*, introd. p. xxi.
7. J. S. Moffat, *The Lives of Robert and Mary Moffat*, p. 16.
8. Robert Moffat, *Missionary Labours*, p. 244.
9. John Philip, *Researches in South Africa*, vol. II, p. 114.

CHAPTER III

1. E. A. Walker, *The Great Trek*; J. A. I. Agar-Hamilton, *The Native Policy of the Voortrekkers*; C. W. de Kiewiet, *A History of South Africa*, chapters I–III.
2. de Kiewiet, *History*, p. 17.
3. There were not many slaves in the pastoral areas: 'The farther from Cape Town the fewer the slaves' (Walker, *The Great Trek*, p. 76).
4. Ibid., pp. 65–6
5. Ibid., chapter I.
6. *Missionary Travels and Researches in South Africa*, p. 30. In the passages relating to Livingstone, Setshele and the Boers, I have made free use of my *Sechele: the story of an African chief*.
7. There has been some controversy as to who pillaged the mission. Paul Kruger, future President of the South African Republic, who took part in the raid as second in command, merely says that the commando 'confiscated the missionary's arsenal'. For this, he says, the Boers 'were abused by Livingstone throughout the length and breadth of England' (*Memoirs*, vol. I, p. 44). Livingstone himself was not at Kolobeng at the time of the raid. The question is discussed by Agar-Hamilton who suggests that much of the damage may have been done by unknown marauders, either Boers or Griqua (*The Native Policy of the Voortrekkers*, p. 152).
8. For the books by Chapman, Gordon Cumming and Baldwin, see Bibliography. For short biographies of a very large number of early travellers and traders, see E. C. Tabler, *Pioneers of Rhodesia*.

CHAPTER IV

1. *Missionary Correspondence*, pp. 171, 175.
2. For the story of this disaster, see Edwin Smith, *Great Lion of Bechuanaland*.
3. For his life, see Anthony Sillery, *John Mackenzie of Bechuanaland*.
4. His story is in *Ten Years North of the Orange River*, chapters XXI–XXIII. Hers is in the London Missionary Society *Chronicle* for July 1866.

5. Parliamentary Papers (P.P.) 1868–9 XLIII 4141, p. 21.
6. P.P.1882 XXVIII C.-3114, Report of the Transvaal Royal Commission, pp. 20–1.
7. Ibid., pp. 88–9. For Lieutenant-Colonel Moysey see p. 51.
8. A. Keppel-Jones, *South Africa*, p. 94.
9. John Mackenzie, *Austral Africa: losing it or ruling it*, vol. I, pp. 116–17.
10. African 86.
11. C.O.48/469 Barkly 53 of 23 May 1874.
12. *Austral Africa*, vol. I, p. 76.
13. P.P.1871 XLVII C.-459, pp. 28–9.
14. P.P.1872 XLIII C.-508, p. 61.
15. C.O.48/494 Frere, 176 of 27 July 1880.
16. P.P.1882 XLVII C.-3381, pp. 73, 98.
17. P.P.1868–9 XLIII 4141, p. 24.
18. Ibid., p. 22.
19. African 110, p. 109.
20. On Barkly 5 of 15 January 1874 (C.O.48/468).
21. P.P.1881 LXVI C.-2754.
22. The Keate Award is in P.P.1872 XLIII C.-508, pp. 26–7.
23. *Oxford History of South Africa*, vol. II, p. 257.
24. P.P.1882 XXVIII C.-3114, Report of the Transvaal Royal Commission, p. 89.
25. C.O.48/468 Barkly 24 of 4 March 1874, minutes.
26. *The Road to the North*, pp. 111–12.
27. *Austral Africa*, vol. I, p. 81.
28. P.P.1882 XLVII C.-3098, p. 45.
29. C.O.291/11 Robinson, telegram 4 August 1881.
30. P.P.1882 XXVIII C.-3114, Report of the Transvaal Royal Commission, p. 22.
31. *Austral Africa*, vol. I, pp. 117–18.

CHAPTER V

1. *Austral Africa*, vol. II, p. 475.
2. Ibid., vol. II, p. 478.
3. Ibid., vol. II, p. 502.
4. Ibid., vol. II, p. 461.
5. Ibid., vol. I, p. 120.
6. Ibid., vol. I, p. 125.
7. P.P.1882 XLVII C.-3098, p. 160.
8. P.P.1882 XLVII C.-3381, p. 4.
9. Ibid., pp. 102, 139.

10. P.P.1882, XLVII C.-3419, pp. 24, 54 et seq., 76.

11. P.P.1882 XLVII C.-3381, p. 147.

12. On Robinson 84 of 5 May 1882 (C.O.291/15).

13. On Robinson 157 of 7 August 1882 (C.O.291/16).

14. P.P.1883 XLIX C.-3486, p. 71.

15. *Pall Mall Gazette*, 13 March 1884.

16. P.P.1882 XLVII C.-3098, p. 95.

17. P.P.1884 LVII C.-3841, p. 104.

18. For the best account of the negotiations leading to the London Convention, the issues involved and the motives of the participants, see D. M. Schreuder, *Gladstone and Kruger*, especially chapters VI and VII.

19. P.P.1884 LVII C.-4036, pp. 34 et seq.

20. Agar-Hamilton, *The Road to the North*, p. 230.

21. C.O.417/6 Warren, telegram 27 July 1885, minutes.

22. African (South) 380. The occasion for this utterance was his farewell speech in Cape Town in April 1889.

23. Agar-Hamilton, *The Road to the North*; Sillery, *John Mackenzie*.

CHAPTER VI

1. P.P.1884 LVII C.-3841, p. 2.

2. Robert Moffat, *Missionary Labours*, p. 229.

3. Tabler, *The Far Interior*, p. 173.

4. Ibid., pp. 172, 175.

5. P.P.1886 XLVIII C.-4643, p. 104.

6. P.P.1884–5 LV C.-4227, p. 4.

7. P.P.1884–5 LVII C.-4432, p. 48.

8. P.P.1878–9 LII C.-2220, p. 55.

9. The Warren and Robinson plans are in P.P.1884–5 LVII C.-4588.

10. Mackenzie to Dale, 19 November 1884, Mackenzie Papers.

11. *Austral Africa*, vol. II, p. 392.

CHAPTER VII

1. African 320.

2. C.O.417/16 Robinson 382 of 19 October 1887, minutes.

3. Shippard's article 'Bechuanaland' in *British Africa*.

4. The report of Shippard's enquiry is in P.P.1890 LI C.-5918.

5. P.P.1890 LI C.-5918, p. 196. For Mackenzie's many prophetic warnings against allowing the Company to administer African peoples, see Sillery, *John Mackenzie*, chapter XIV.

6. African (South) 372, p. 71: Colonial Office to Foreign Office,

16 May 1889. Lord Knutsford was Secretary of State for the Colonies 1887–92.

7. C.O.417/27 Robinson 63 of 25 January 1889.

8. Shippard's report of the meeting, dated 6 February 1889, is enclosed in Robinson's confidential despatch of 27 February 1889 (C.O.417/28).

9. Claire Palley, *The Constitutional History and Law of Southern Rhodesia*, p. 38.

CHAPTER VIII

1. C.O.417/139 Loch 118 of 19 March 1895, enclosure.

2. Shippard's arbitration is in Robinson 395 of 29 July 1895 (C.O.417/141).

3. *The Gay-Dombeys*, p. 210.

4. See Schapera, 'The native land problem in the Tati District', *Botswana Notes and Records*, vol. 3.

5. Margery Perham, *Lugard: the Years of Adventure*, pp. 561–620.

6. C.O.417/114 Loch 153 of 13 March 1894, minutes.

7. For an account of the Ghanzi trek, see *The Round Table*, nos. 65 and 74, 'The Great Ngami Trek'; 'After the Great Ngami Trek'.

8. See Schapera, 'Report on the system of land tenure in the Barolong Farms' (Botswana National Archives (BNA) S.168/3); also references in the same author's *Native Land Tenure in the Bechuanaland Protectorate*.

CHAPTER IX

1. African (South) 484, p. 74.

2. *The Sunday Times*, 6 October 1895.

3. Ibid.

4. For the chiefs' visit to England and their negotiations with Chamberlain, see P.P.1896 LIX C.-7962.

5. *Native Administration in the British African Territories*, part V, pp. 200–1.

CHAPTER X

1. *Annual Report, 1896–7*.

2. Hailey, *Native Administration in the British African Territories*, part V, p. 324.

3. See for instance Sillery, *Founding a Protectorate*, p. 114.

4. C.O.417/44 Loch 491 of 1890.

5. In a paper read to the Institute of Commonwealth Studies, London University, in March 1971, Neil Parsons quotes a letter

of October 1893 from Khama complaining that a 'ruler' (Moffat) had been placed in Palapye 'so that I myself, before I can buy a bag of gun-powder, have to go and obtain a permit'.

6. Ibid.
7. Sillery, *The Bechuanaland Protectorate*, p. 126.
8. Ibid., pp. 146–7.
9. There has been some controversy on the Derdepoort affair, particularly as to why the Kgatla took part in the action in contravention of Surmon's instructions that they should not go beyond the Protectorate frontier. See Hickman, *Rhodesia Served the Queen*, pp. 233 et seq.; Sillery, *The Bechuanaland Protectorate*, p. 92.
10. Quoted in Lord Hailey, *The Republic of South Africa and the High Commission Territories*, pp. 29, 33.
11. Cmd.8707, pp. 46 et seq.

CHAPTER XI

1. Appeal No. 4 of 1930.
2. *Official Gazette*, 4 January 1935.
3. For Mr Justice Watermeyer's judgement, see the High Commission Territories Law Reports 1926–53, pp. 9 et seq., Tshekedi Khama and another vs. High Commissioner.
4. Hailey, *Native Administration in the British African Territories*, part V, p. 222.
5. For more on this subject see Schapera, *Tribal Innovators 1795–1940*.
6. Hailey, *Native Administration*, p. 222.

CHAPTER XII

1. *Travels*, vol. II, pp. 409–11.
2. Bailie's reports are of great historical interest. They are in P.P.1878–9 LII C.-2220.
3. *Report on the Population Census* 1971, pp. 113–14.
4. C.O.417/252 Treasury, 11 November 1898.
5. Cmd.4368, 1932–3.

CHAPTER XIII

1. Field-Marshal J. C. Smuts. Quoted in Mary Benson, *Tshekedi Khama*, p. 200.
2. *Basutoland, Bechuanaland Protectorate and Swaziland: Report of an Economic Survey Mission*.

CHAPTER XV

1. *The Human Land and Water Resources of the Shoshong Area, Eastern Botswana*, vol. I. The quotations are from pp. 17 and 147.

2. Ibid., p. 176.

3. In his book *Okavango Adventure*, the experienced Wilmot suggests very strongly that the smaller carnivores are man's best allies against plague-carrying rodents. Wilmot himself witnessed an outbreak of plague at Maun in 1944.

4. *2000 Million Poor.*

5. *National Development Plan 1970–75*, pp. 48, 100.

6. Ibid., foreword.

7. For the difficulties facing any programme of rural regeneration, see Fosbrooke, note 1 above.

8. *National Development Plan 1970–75*, p. 134.

9. Ibid.

10. J. E. S. Griffiths, 'A note on local government in Botswana' (*Botswana Notes and Records*, vol. 2), makes useful reading.

11. *National Development Plan 1970–75*, p. 18.

Sources and Bibliography

I. PRIMARY

1. Public Record Office: C.O.48, C.O.291, C.O.417. These contain the correspondence between the British High Commissioner in South Africa and the Colonial Office, together with the relevant Colonial Office minutes. They also include questions asked in Parliament, the replies on subjects within the High Commissioner's orbit, and correspondence with other departments and with companies and individuals on matters arising in regions for which the High Commissioner was responsible
2. London Missionary Society (Congregational Council for World Mission, London): in-letters, South Africa. Letters and reports from the missionaries in the field.
3. Botswana National Archives. These are in Gaborone, Botswana. They are very well kept and contain much material not available elsewhere.
4. *Mackenzie Papers*, Witwatersrand University Library.

II. OFFICIAL PRINTS AND PUBLICATIONS, REPORTS ETC.

1. Colonial Office Confidential Prints, African and African (South): 86, 110, 320, 372, 380, 484.
2. Parliamentary Papers

1868–9	XLIII	4141
1871	XLVII	C.-459
1872	XLIII	C.-508
1878–9	LII	C.-2220
1881	LXVI	C.-2754
1882	XLVII	C.-3098, C.-3381, C.-3419
1882	XXVIII	C.-3114, C.-3219
1883	XLIX	C.-3486
1884	LVII	C.-3841, C.-4036
1884–5	LV	C.-4227
1884–5	LVII	C.-4432, C.-4588
1886	XLVIII	C.-4643

1890   LI   C.-5918
1896   LIX   C.-7962.

1932–3 X Cmd.4368. Financial and Economic Position of the Bechuanaland Protectorate ('The Pim Report').

1950 XIX Cmd.7913. Succession to the Chieftainship of the Bamangwato Tribe.

1951–2 IX Cmd.8423. Reports of observers on the attitude of the Bamangwato Tribe to the return of Tshekedi Khama to the Bamangwato Reserve.

1952–3 XXIII Cmd. 8707. History of discussions with the Union of South Africa 1909–1939 (the transfer question).

1959–60 XXVII Cmd.1159. Bechuanaland Protectorate Constitutional Proposals.

1963–4 XXV Cmd.2378. Bechuanaland Constitutional Proposals.

1965–6 V Cmd.2929. Report of the Bechuanaland Independence Conference, 1966.

1966–7 I Botswana Independence Bill 1966.

3. *Bechuanaland Protectorate Annual Reports.*

4. *High Commission Territories Law Reports 1926–53.*

5. *High Commissioner's Notices and Proclamations.*

6. Minutes of the Native (African), European and Joint Advisory Councils.

7. *Basutoland, Bechuanaland Protectorate and Swaziland: Report of an Economic Survey Mission*, London, HMSO, 1960.

8. Silberbauer, G. B., *Report to the Government of Bechuanaland on the Bushman Survey*, Bechuanaland Government, 1965.

9. *National Development Plan 1970–75*, Gaborone, Government Printer, September 1970.

10. *Report on the Population Census 1971*, Gaborone, Central Statistics Office.

11. a. *Financial Statements, Tables and Estimates of Recurrent Revenue 1972–3.*

    b. *Estimates of Recurrent Expenditure 1972–3.*

    c. *Estimates of Revenue and Expenditure for the Development Fund 1972–3.*

12. Fosbrooke, H. A., *The Human, Land and Water Resources of the Shoshong Area, Eastern Botswana.* A paper produced in connection with a survey sponsored by the Food and Agricultural Organization of the United Nations.

III. PRINTED BOOKS, PERIODICALS

Agar-Hamilton, J. A. I., *The Native Policy of the Voortrekkers*, Cape Town, Maskew Miller, 1928.

——, *The Road to the North*, London, Longmans, Green & Co., 1937. Deservedly the best-known book on the advance of the European into Bechuanaland.

Baldwin, W. C., *African Hunting from Natal to the Zambezi*, London, Richard Bentley, 1863. The toll of animal life is dreadful, but there are good descriptions of the contemporary scene.

Barrow, John, *A voyage to Cochin-China in the years 1792 and 1793*, London, T. Cadell & W. Davies, 1806. This contains as an annex, under the title *An account of a journey to Leetakoo*, the report of the Trüter–Somerville expedition to the capital of the Tlhaping in 1801.

Benson, Mary, *Tshekedi Khama*, London, Faber & Faber, 1960. The sources are too restricted and the story of Tshekedi's many brushes with the British authorities is therefore one-sided. However, the author knew Tshekedi well, and the book gives a vivid picture of this remarkable man.

Bent, R. A. R., *Ten Thousand Men of Africa*, London, HMSO, 1952. Tswana troops in the Second World War by one who served with them.

Botswana Notes and Records, Botswana Society, Gaborone. An annual periodical containing many articles of current and historical interest.

Breutz, P.-L., *The Tribes of Vryburg District*, Pretoria, 1959. One of a series of useful publications by the Department of Bantu Administration and Development.

Brown, J. T., *Among the Bantu Nomads*, London, Seeley, Service & Co., 1926. A well-known account of the Tswana tribes, especially the southern ones.

Burchell, W. J., *Travels in the Interior of South Africa*, London, Batchworth Press, 1953, 2 vols. A reprint of Burchell's classic originally published in 1822. Nearly half of the second volume is devoted to the Tlhaping.

Campbell, John, *Travels in South Africa undertaken at the request of the Missionary Society*, London, Black & Parry, 1815. Campbell it was who prepared the way for the coming of the missionaries.

Chapman, James, *Travels in the Interior of South Africa*, London, Bell & Daldy; Edward Stanford, 1868, 2 vols. 'Chapman was the greatest of South African pioneers of his period, owing to his wide range of interests and his powers of observation, which were the equal of Livingstone's' (Tabler, *Pioneers of Rhodesia*).

Cole, D. T., *Introduction to Tswana Grammar*, London, Longman's, Green, 1955.

Cumming, R. Gordon, *A Hunter's Life in South Africa*, London, John Murray, 1850. Mainly devoted to the slaughter of big game, but contains useful descriptions of mid-century Bechuanaland and of some leading personalities.

Hailey, Lord, *Native Administration in the British African Territories*, Part V, London, HMSO, 1953. This part deals with the High Commission Territories.

——, *The Republic of South Africa and the High Commission Territories*, London, Oxford University Press, 1963. The question of transfer.

Hearst, Stephen, *2000 Million Poor*, London, Harrap, 1965.

Hepburn, J. D., *Twenty Years in Khama's Country*, London, Hodder & Stoughton, 1895. Contains, *inter alia*, a description of the establishment and failure of the first Ngamiland Church.

Hickman, A. S., *Rhodesia served the Queen*, Government of Rhodesia, 1970. Rhodesian forces in the Boer War. Of special relevance to the eastern frontier of Bechuanaland.

Hyman, Ronald, *The Failure of South African Expansion 1908–1948*, London, Macmillan, 1972. The latest and most detailed study of the transfer issue.

Johnston, Sir Harry, *The Gay-Dombeys*, London, Chatto & Windus, 1919. A very odd autobiographical novel. Eminent people connected with colonial affairs appear in thin disguise.

Keppel-Jones, A., *South Africa*, London, Hutchinson, 1966.

Kiewiet, C. W. de, *A History of South Africa, Social and Economic*, London, Oxford University Press, 1941.

Kruger, Paul, *The Memoirs of Paul Kruger*, London, T. Fisher Unwin, 1902, 2 vols.

Lichtenstein, Henry, *Travels in Southern Africa in the years 1803, 1804, 1805 and 1806*, Cape Town, van Riebeeck Society, 1928, 2 vols. Sympathetic and lively account of the southern Tswana by an early visitor.

Livingstone, David, *Missionary Travels and Researches in South Africa*, London, John Murray, 1857. Livingstone's famous book contains an account of chief Setshele's troubles with the Boers, the discovery of Lake Ngami, and ends with Livingstone's arrival at Quilimane in 1856 after crossing the continent from west to east.

——, *Missionary Correspondence 1841–1856*, ed. Isaac Schapera,

London, Chatto & Windus, 1961. The value of this correspondence is much enhanced by Schapera's excellent introduction and his detailed footnotes.

Lloyd, Edwin, *Three great African Chiefs*, London, T. Fisher Unwin, 1895. The chiefs are Khama, Sebele and Bathoen.

Lockhart, J. G. and Woodhouse, C. M., *Rhodes*, London, Hodder & Stoughton, 1963. The latest biography.

Lovett, Richard, *The History of the London Missionary Society, 1795–1895*, London, Henry Frowde, 1899, 2 vols.

Mackenzie, John, *Ten Years North of the Orange River*, Edinburgh, Edmonston & Douglas, 1871. Mackenzie's experiences as a missionary before his direct involvement in politics. It includes an account of the rescue by him of the survivors of the Helmore–Price expedition.

——, *Austral Africa: losing it or ruling it*, London, Sampson Low, Marston, Searle & Rivington, 1887, 2 vols. Mackenzie's weighty *apologia pro vita sua*, containing a statement of his tenaciously-held opinions on the government of African territories, the story of his campaigns for British administration in Bechuanaland, and an account of his own tenure of the office of Deputy Commissioner.

Moffat, J. S., *The Lives of Robert and Mary Moffat*, London, T. Fisher Unwin, 1885.

Moffat, Robert, *Missionary Labours and Scenes in Southern Africa*, London, John Snow, 1842. The establishment of the mission at Kuruman and incidents in a missionary's life.

——, *Apprenticeship at Kuruman*, London, Chatto & Windus, 1951. The journals and letters of Robert and Mary Moffat 1820–8. The volume forms part of the Oppenheimer series, Central African Archives. Schapera's editing adds substantially to its value.

Molema, S. M., *Montshiwa, Barolong Chief and Patriot*, Cape Town, Struik, 1966. The author was himself a member of the Rolong chiefly family.

Munger, F. S., *Bechuanaland: Pan-African Outpost or Bantu Homeland?*, London, Oxford University Press, 1965. Useful background to recent history.

Oxford History of South Africa, Oxford, Clarendon Press, 1969 and 1971, 2 vols.

Palley, Claire, *The Constitutional History and Law of Southern Rhodesia*, Oxford, Clarendon Press, 1966.

Perham, M. F., *Lugard: The Years of Adventure*, London, Collins, 1956. For Lugard's venture into Ngamiland.

Philip, John, *Researches in South Africa*, London, James Duncan,

1828, 2 vols. Philip includes in this, his famous polemical work, a description of Kuruman.

Price, E. L., *The Journals of Elizabeth Lees Price*, ed. Una Long. London, Edward Arnold, 1956. Elizabeth Price was a daughter of Robert Moffat and second wife of Roger Price. These journals give a detailed picture of the life of a missionary family and are particularly interesting in the light which they throw on chief Setshele, whom the Prices knew well.

Round Table, The, No. 65, December 1926, 'The Great Ngami Trek'.

——, No. 74, March 1929, 'After the Great Ngami Trek'.

——, No. 106, March 1937, 'The Crown and the Bechuanaland Protectorate'. Discusses the case in which Tshekedi and Bathoen challenge the Proclamations of 1934.

Schapera, Isaac, *A Handbook of Tswana Law and Custom*, London, Oxford University Press, 2nd ed., 1955.

——, *Native Land Tenure in the Bechuanaland Protectorate*, South Africa, Lovedale Press, 1943.

——, *Migrant Labour and Tribal Life*, London, Oxford University Press, 1947.

——, *The Ethnic Composition of the Tswana Tribes*, London School of Economics and Political Science, 1952.

——, *The Tswana*, London, International African Institute, 1953.

——, *Tribal Innovators 1795–1940*, London, Athlone Press, 1970. The chiefs as initiators of reform and change.

All Schapera's books are essential reading for the student of Botswana.

Schreuder, D. M., *Gladstone and Kruger*, London, Routledge & Kegan Paul, 1969. The higher politics of the Transvaal border in the 'eighties. The standard work on the subject.

Shippard, S. G. A., 'Bechuanaland', an article in *British Africa*, London, Kegan Paul, Trench, Trübner, & Co., 1899.

Sillery, Anthony, *The Bechuanaland Protectorate*, Cape Town, Oxford University Press, 1952. General and tribal history.

——, *Founding a Protectorate*, The Hague, Mouton, 1965. The Bechuanaland Protectorate 1885–95.

——, *John Mackenzie of Bechuanaland*, Cape Town, Balkema, 1971. A political biography.

Smit, P., *Botswana: Resources and Development*, Pretoria, Africa Institute of South Africa, 1970. Clear and factual.

Smith, Edwin, *Great Lion of Bechuanaland*, London, Independent Press, 1957. The life of the missionary Roger Price.

Stevens, R. P., *Lesotho, Botswana and Swaziland*, London, Pall Mall Press, 1967. Concise and informative.

Tabler, E. C., *The Far Interior*, Cape Town, Balkema, 1955.

——, *Pioneers of Rhodesia*, Cape Town, Struik, 1966.

These books between them are a mine of information about the 'Road to the North', the men who trod it and the people who lived along it.

Thomas, E. M., *The Harmless People*, London, Secker & Warburg, 1959. The 'harmless people' are the Bushmen.

Thompson, George, *Travels and Adventures in Southern Africa*, London, Henry Colburn, 1827, 2 vols. Thompson was at Kuruman in 1823, and his description of a tribal war council is famous.

Walker, E. A., *The Great Trek*, London, Adam and Charles Black, 2nd ed., 1938.

——, *A History of Southern Africa*, London, Longmans, Green & Co., 1957.

Both are standard works, the latter an indispensable one.

Williams, Watkin W., *The Life of Sir Charles Warren*, Oxford, Basil Blackwell, 1941. Biography of a man who played a leading part in establishing the Protectorate.

Wilmot, E. C., *Okavango Adventure*, Cape Town, Howard Timmins, 1970. An unusual book about a fascinating part of the country.

The following bibliographies are also recommended:

Brownlee, Margaret, *The Lives and Work of South African Missionaries*, 1969.

Middleton, Coral, *Bechuanaland*, 1965.

Stevens, Pamela E., *Bechuanaland*, 1969.

They are all published by the University of Cape Town Libraries.

Index